Whistleblower

Whistleblower

January 28, 2011
To Joan,
For truth and justice!

[signature]

Amy Block Joy

Bay Tree Publishing, LLC
Point Richmond California

Library of Congress Cataloging-in-Publication Data

Joy, Amy Block.
  Whistleblower / Amy Block Joy.
    p. cm.
  Includes bibliographical references.
  ISBN 978-0-9819577-4-6
1. Universities and colleges--Corrupt practices--United States. 2. Education, Higher--Moral and ethical aspects--United States. I. Title.
  LB3609.J65 2010
  378.794'51--dc22
  [B]
                            2010031255

For my muse in shining armor whose wisdom
is infused throughout this book.

Thank you for believing in me.

ॐ

Contents

Author's Note

Whistleblower is my personal account of the discovery and reporting of crime. The events and conversations reported are based on my recollection and on articles, interviews, and documents that I have reviewed. Names and identifying characteristics of some of the people involved have been changed.

I wrote this book to educate future whistleblowers, especially those in university settings. My advice: persist, be vigilant, and know that an individual can make a difference.

Foreword

When I first met Dr. Amy Block Joy in our law offices in 2006, I could tell this much right away: she was in trouble. She sat rigidly at our cherrywood conference table in downtown Sacramento, surrounded by an associate, an investigator from our firm, and me. She appeared intelligent, poised, articulate ... and terrified. I didn't tell her at the time, but she had good reason to be. Dr. Block Joy had become a whistleblower.

I represent whistleblowers for a living. For fifteen years at the U.S. Attorney's office, where I was a prosecutor and then a supervising prosecutor for the United States, I worked regularly with them. They were often important witnesses. Yet until I started representing them in private practice—until they confided in me as their personal lawyer—I had only the most basic understanding of what whistleblowers endure. I had a stronger appreciation for the millions of dollars these individuals can earn by blowing the whistle.

Money, indeed, remains at the center of every fraud case, and the government has capitalized on this for years. The country's oldest and best tool to prosecute these cases, the False Claims Act, was enacted in 1863 to stop fraud by Civil War profiteers. From its earliest days and through a series of amendments, the False Claims Act has dangled a financial incentive before whistleblowers. File a secret complaint under seal, tell the government what you know, and you can share in the government's triple damages recovery in a fraud case. The formula has proven successful: from October 1987 through the end of the last fiscal year, Department of Justice statistics show fraud recoveries of over $15.6 billion in whistleblower cases. In those actions, whistleblowers themselves have earned almost $2.5 billion.

What's never reflected in the statistics is the potential toll on those who blow the whistle. The False Claims Act tries to protect whistleblowers from harassment by further awarding double damages, plus interest, against employers and others who retaliate against them. Still, for some, a share of the overall fraud recovery and personal damages for retaliation doesn't compensate for the risk of exposing the fraud.

Dr. Block Joy's story is an unflinching account inside the life of a whistleblower. Told with intensity and a sometimes heartbreaking honesty, it reveals much about the ugly underside of friendship and money. As it turns out, with millions of dollars at stake, academics don't act much differently than businessmen, who don't act much differently than the rest of us. Though astonished by the malice of friends whom she thought would praise her discovery and reporting of the fraud, perhaps Dr. Block Joy shouldn't have been surprised. Retaliation against whistleblowers is embedded in our culture. While we're taught as children to "do the right thing," we're also taught that "no one likes a tattletale."

So be forewarned if you blow the whistle long, loud, and without being silenced, as Amy did. If you think many colleagues you like, admire, and trust will react favorably, Dr. Block Joy's story will make you think again. Your friends and colleagues who committed the fraud may be prosecuted; those who gained from the fraud may be ruined financially; and even those not involved in the fraud will find the reputation of the entity for which they work discredited—as such, their own reputation and marketability may be tainted, as well. For many, gratitude is the one response you can safely rule out.

Yet, like Amy, whistleblowers can also find admirers: people who genuinely prize integrity and courage in their colleagues.

As Amy found, admirers can become supporters and eventually true friends, often from sources a whistleblower never expects.

The False Claims Act did not apply to Amy's case, but other remedies were available. While representing Dr. Block Joy in her successful retaliation complaint against the University of California, I saw her determination reinforced by the support of friends in unlikely places. I also saw the criticism, betrayal, and abuse she endured. After all of it, I've never asked Amy whether she was happy she blew the whistle. I've never dared.

Michael A. Hirst, Esq.
Hirst Law Group, P.C.
Sacramento, California

1 | Police

"Embezzlement cannot be tolerated by the University."

The words I had written six months ago in a confidential letter to my boss—my first act as a whistleblower—echoed through my mind as I sat perched on the edge of a folding chair facing the lieutenant detective at the University of California at Davis police station. Seated at one end of a large rectangular table, he was writing, his eyes on the papers in front of him. A steel reinforced tempered window behind me was closed.

The sun was heating up the interview room. I waited silently for the detective to complete the paperwork. I had already been alone in the room for at least thirty minutes, sitting on pins and needles, worrying about my impending interview.

I had been warned earlier in the week by the assistant executive vice-chancellor, or as he was called, the locally designated official (LDO) for UC Davis. "I ask that you not discuss these matters with anyone," he wrote in an ominous-sounding letter delivered to my home by one of the UC Davis college deans, someone I had considered a friend. The dean showed up at my house, instructed me to read the letter out loud to him, listened stone-faced in my driveway, then asked me to sign a form that stated that I had been "served." This driveway incident was just one of many that had made me distrust everyone. Many folks I had worked with for years and whom I had also believed were friends were now avoiding me.

I looked up whistleblowers on the Internet. Most of the stories had the same ending: Fired! Reading such tales filled with financial ruin, chronic stress, marital conflict, workplace hostility, and ongoing harassment had been keeping me up at night. Worried that my career was over, the thought of an unknown future frightened me. Beads of sweat formed on my forehead as I agonized silently in that room at the station.

From the moment he sat down, the detective hadn't taken his eyes off the papers. I kept waiting for some eye contact between us. I wanted to smile at him and see if he returned the smile. Although I knew it was rude to stare, I wanted to know if he was going to believe me.

I had received an email from his assistant the day before. I stared for a long time at the email before I replied to confirm this interview. The email wasn't particularly alarming, although it was the first one I had ever received from a police department. I pondered a long time if I should say "thank you" at the end of my reply. I decided to do exactly the same as the officer's assistant who sent it to me. There was no "sincerely," no "thank you," no "regards;" just a signature line. I found a picture and a short bio of the detective on the campus Web site. He was smiling in the picture. I pictured him smiling at me. Yet, there he sat a few feet away from me with his head buried in papers. I felt a large empty space, a void, a black hole that separated us and made my heart race.

There was a tape recorder in the middle of the table. Another officer, quite tall, entered the room, gave me a brief, friendly nod, took a seat near the tape recorder, and handed a tape to the detective. His uniform was stretched tightly over his shoulders. A stream of words was coming out of his mouth, and I struggled to follow. His voice was deep, and he was speaking in what sounded like police code. He was whispering to the detective, but I was close enough to hear every word. It all sounded more like white noise, so I took a deep breath, sat bolt upright, and felt some long-lost feeling stirring inside me.

The sound of plastic wrap being ripped off the tape startled me. I heard a car honking outside the room. Pushing the sounds and stirrings aside, I turned my full attention to the detective, who finally lifted his head, glanced at me with a poker face, moved the recorder closer to my side of the table, and inserted the tape. A third police detective, also in uniform, entered the room, shut the door with a loud clang, and handed a microphone to the detective. He plugged it into the recorder, positioned it next to me, and signaled that the tape was rolling. He turned to me with a slight nod and then began speaking.

"This is an interview with Amy Block Joy. Please state, then spell, your name, working title, address, and telephone number, speaking slowly and clearly."

I moved my chair closer to the microphone. In one breath, I said my name, then spelled it. My title, address, and telephone number followed. I noted that the light in the room seemed to dim and that I had become fully aware of every nuance. The light on the recorder lit up with each spoken word. One of the detectives had a coughing spell, and I stopped talking; I reached for my purse to offer him a cough drop, then realized that my purse was somewhere else. I suddenly was brought back to the fact that I was in a small room with the police! The room seemed to be getting smaller as my heart kept pounding. What would my daughter say when I told her that I had been interviewed by the police?

"How long have you worked for the University of California?"

"Twenty-eight years," I answered.

I wanted to add that I had been at UC Davis only fourteen of those years. I wondered if it mattered. Did my years of service as a member of the faculty mean anything? Would my past dedication to public service help me?

My mind flashed back to how obsessed I had been about what to wear to this interview. After receiving that email, I searched my closet and realized that all my clothes were pretty much the same—all business suits made by Jones of New York. These suits fit me perfectly, and I liked the image they projected—businesslike and professional. After all, I was the director of a $14 million statewide program. After much deliberation, I selected a navy-blue, pinstriped, two-piece tailored suit.

At work, before the interview, one of my staff teased me. She said I was wearing "jail-house garb" in reference to the stripes. I smiled and forced a laugh, then became paranoid, afraid she had found out that I was on my way to the police station. I left my office wondering if everyone knew. I felt a familiar pain of being left in the dark.

As I got into my car, I began obsessing about whether the police email had said "interview" or "interrogation." Did I miss something critical? I wanted to stop and read it again. My mind became so preoccupied with the one sentence email that the minute I arrived at the parking lot, I found my printed copy of the email and read it again. I was relieved to confirm that the email clearly said "interview."

The detective cleared his throat. I had been staring into space, beginning to feel disoriented. He moved a little in his chair, and I wondered if he was becoming impatient.

"What kind of work do you do for UC?"

More comfortable with this and other general questions, I started to feel more confident. The sound of the tape turning in the recorder became a blur that no longer captivated my attention. I talked at length about my accomplishments over the years. I told the police, "I value hard work and I consider my twenty-eight-year university career to be one of great dedication and passion."

For the next two hours, I continued to answer questions. As I spoke, I noted that the detective was shuffling papers, and I saw that he had pulled one file out of the stack. He opened it and handed me a two-page letter. Without much fanfare, he asked me to look at it.

"Is this your letter? Is that your signature?"

"Yes."

I didn't need to study this whistleblowing letter; it was already seared onto my brain. I had written it then rewritten it many times, and my words had been carefully chosen. "Embezzlement cannot be tolerated by the University" was highlighted in yellow on the copy he handed to me, on which he had also marked in large block letters across the top, "EXHIBIT 1."

As if struck by lightning, the room suddenly became ablaze with energy, and I felt electrically charged. The detective, now more attentive and energetic, stared straight at me. He asked me specifically about a particular day in March 2006. Although that was six months before, I had no trouble remembering the specifics of that day. March 2, 2006 was the day of my sudden appearance in the spotlight.

My heart started beating wildly as my eyes met his. For twenty-eight years, my career as a scientist had been completely uncontroversial. Now, perched on the edge of my seat, feeling numb, I began to wonder about the "big picture." His face revealed nothing.

"Who did you write this letter to?"

"My supervisor."

A wave of nausea swept over me when the detective asked me about my supervisor. I responded, "My supervisor is a highly regarded and famous scientist. He has served as the department chair as well as an endowed chair at the medical school for the last fifteen years."

The detective wasn't impressed. He asked, "Did your supervisor agree with your letter?"

My thoughts returned to that fateful day in March when I handed the chair my letter. He took it and leaned back, his fingers tapping nervously on his gray leather swivel chair. Short and stocky, he kept the chair higher that the other chairs in his office so that he could look down on those he was talking to.

I couldn't speak for a moment; the detective waited for me to answer his question. My skin was crawling.

I began to worry that I was responding too slowly, and I was having real difficulty remembering the question. Not wanting to ask the detective to repeat it, I found myself babbling a little too loudly about how my supervisor's fingers were drumming on his chair, as though his rhythm had some unmistakable meaning. My voice, squeaky and rapid, stopped abruptly.

Finally, at least partially answering the question, I concluded with the statement that I believed my supervisor felt the same way that I did.

"Yes. He agreed with me during the March 2 meeting."

"Are you sure?"

I looked up, astonished. Those were the exact words the chair had used the day after I gave him the letter!

"I wasn't sure. I was puzzled and worried by his behavior toward me."

"Describe his behavior . . . better yet, what was your relationship with your supervisor?"

"He was held in high regard. His power and authority loomed large. He was my supervisor. Like everyone else in my department, I was at his mercy. He could get rid of me . . . " I snapped my fingers, "like that!"

I expected the detective to nod, encourage me to continue, or even signal that he understood. I became perplexed again by his unemotional response. His next question came quickly.

"When did you decide to blow the whistle?"

I imagined he was watching my eyes as I thought about this question, and I became self-conscious, fearing I was taking way too long to think about this. I again began to feel that stirring of fear and anxiety that had passed over me just before the interview began. I tried to answer quickly. Words tumbled out of my mouth.

"I wanted to be sure. I wanted to feel confident that I was correct in my assessment. I wanted to make sure that I had covered all my bases. I wanted to double-check, recheck, verify all the information that I'd collected. I wanted my evidence to be indisputable, unequivocal. I wanted to nail it. Oh . . . sorry." I stopped, suddenly realizing that I was going on and on and probably sounding unsure.

"I haven't answered your question," I continued. His was a question about timing, not a why question. "I decided . . . well, maybe decided isn't really the correct word." I thought for a few seconds. The clock on the wall seemed to be ticking much slower than my own heart.

"I became determined . . . Oh, your question was 'when'... hmm . . . after my third attempt to notify the chair about what I found."

"What did you find?" The tape whizzed in the background as I felt a rush of adrenaline.

"I found embezzlement," I answered. Looking directly at the detective, I continued. "I sent the chair three letters containing evidence. You have the first one right there." I pointed to my letter. "He ignored all my attempts to follow policy," I stated matter-of-factly. "So, I notified the vice-chair, requesting his permission to notify someone at the dean's office. He refused to grant me permission and, instead, told me to wait."

Wanting to tell the police everything, I hesitated only to look around the room. "Wait? I couldn't wait another second. I prepared and certified a full whistleblower report and mailed copies to everyone I could think of: the department chair, the vice-chair, and the dean, that same guy who served me in my driveway."

I continued with renewed confidence. "I also sent a copy to the chancellor's office." Suddenly, the room grew very quiet again, and all eyes turned toward me.

I looked directly at the detective and remained calm. "I had a hard time sending it to the chancellor. So I addressed the envelope, 'Chancellor's Office, University of California, Davis, California.' Sending a letter to the chancellor meant going over a lot of people's heads. I was sure I would be hung, hung out to dry, for taking such a dramatic step. I believed this report would be the kiss of death for me and my career. But there was no other option." I rushed to finish. "This was something I had to do and nothing was going to stop me!"

The detective wiped his own forehead vigorously as if to let me know that I was sweating. He didn't have to hold up a mirror. As a bead of sweat started to move down my forehead very slowly, I moved my head away from the light to look again at the other policeman, the smiling one sitting at the other end of the table. He dropped his head slightly as I lifted mine to stop the sweat from falling onto the table. As our eyes met, I experienced a sudden release of tension.

The tape machine clicked and stopped abruptly. The detective quickly said to me, "Hold that thought" as he put in a new tape and started it up again. My heart was pounding.

I was looking at him for a signal to begin. Instead, he said, "This is a continuation of an interview with Amy Block Joy." Then, to me, he said, "What was the chair's response?"

"The chair's response . . . his response to . . ." The whirring sound of the tape made me lose my concentration

The detective repeated his question. "What was his response to your embezzlement notification?"

"He was stunned."

I began to picture him again. This time his eyes were downcast and he looked desolate, almost despondent. He was staring at my letter rather than at me. He had dropped his pen, which came to rest a few inches from his bare feet. He was wearing Birkenstocks, and I saw him shift uncomfortably in his chair, turning slightly away from me, shaking his head in disbelief. I wanted to pick up the pen for him but it was too far from where I was seated, and I was frozen to my chair, unable to move. He remained silent and didn't bother to pick it up.

"Why do you think he was stunned?" The detective was speaking very slowly.

Gathering up all my courage, I sat up and exclaimed, "He was stunned because I had found out!" At that very moment, as I clutched the table at the police station, I realized the chair had given himself away.

The detective turned off the tape recorder. The machine snapped to a stop, startling me.

"Time for a break. I'm going to get a coke." As the detective and the other police detectives left the room, the friendly one caught my eye and asked if I would like some water. I nodded, "Thanks," then turned my head as tears began to form.

"I'll be back in ten minutes," he said quietly with a friendly nod, then left the room and gently shut the door. An inner voice had been silently praying, "Don't leave, don't leave me alone."

I wanted him to comfort me, or just stay with me, or say soothing things. I wanted him to tell me that I was okay, that I was safe and sound. Tears welled up in my eyes. I slowly pushed my chair away from the table.

I wanted to get up and move around the room; I needed to pace. But I forced myself to remain seated as I pondered how this had happened. Why did I become a whistleblower? Why me?

In my mind, I went over what I knew: *I discovered a crime. When I tried to report it, I was stopped by my boss. Why did he want to stop me? What was really going on? Was he involved?*

Gradually, I began to feel a little safer. No longer captive of the ordeal, I relaxed. Glued to the chair, an ancient memory slowly encircled me, forcing me to sit up and take note. A sweet song from my childhood whispered in my ear as I waited for the friendly policeman to return:

"Oh, dream maker, you heart breaker, wherever you're going I'm going your way..."

I didn't tell anyone at work or at home about my September 14, 2006 interview with the police. I kept going over and over Dr. Savage's attempts to silence me. What on earth was he hiding?

2 | **Raymond**

I first met Dr. Raymond Savage, chair of the UC Davis Department of Food, Health and Society, in early 1992, when I drove up to Davis from Berkeley for an early afternoon meeting.

I'd been working as an academic in the university president's office in Oakland for years. Hired on April 1, 1980, I'd been through a number of transitions within the university, including four different job titles, twelve different supervisors, and six offices, five in Berkeley and one in Oakland. In 1992, my stately office on the sixth floor of Oakland's Kaiser Building overlooked Lake Merritt. Although the view from my office window was fantastic, I yearned to return to campus.

On my drive up to Davis, I thought about the new decentralization plan for UC and what my current supervisor, Dr. Gloria Jones, the assistant vice president for agriculture, had advised.

"The president is moving all the academics to Davis. Now is the time to introduce yourself to the department chair, Dr. Raymond Savage," she told me in a serious tone of voice. I understood the message—Dr. Savage had quite a reputation. According to the grapevine, he was considered a superstar at Davis—brilliant, cunning, and effective.

During my hour drive, I rehearsed what I would say.

Hello Dr. Savage, I'm Amy Block Joy. The assistant VP for agriculture, Gloria Jones, urged me to meet with you. She indicated to me that my position may be moved from my Oakland office to your department.

I arrived early at his third-floor office and introduced myself to the chair's very pretty administrative assistant sitting in a cubicle outside his office. She told me that he was expecting me and to go right in. His door was open.

I knocked. He was sitting at his desk in a swivel chair with his back to me as I entered. He turned and then stood up as I walked over to him. We shook hands and he motioned for me to take a seat in his very large and cushy office. African and Asian masks from various countries were displayed on the walls of his office. I had a similar collection in my home.

Dr. Savage wasn't like any professor I'd ever met. He was young and dressed very casually, wearing shorts, a Hawaiian shirt, and flip-flops. I, of course, was dressed in a business suit.

"I thought it'd be good to introduce myself to you," I said confidently. I'd heard he was quite intimidating and I wanted him to see that I wasn't afraid. Before I was able to recite my practiced introduction, he spoke.

"I've read your papers and am impressed with your work." He looked directly at me. I was quite surprised and flattered that he'd taken the time to read my work. Dr. Savage had published hundreds of papers on a wide range of subjects, including nutrition, chemistry, biochemistry, genetics, diabetes, and medicine. I'd studied a number of his publications on glucose metabolism in mice, monkeys, rats, and neonates. He was a well-known, highly respected scientist, and a lot of journals churned out his publications. He also had ties to a number of corporations, which allowed him to bring big bucks to Davis. Very smart and politically astute, he had a youthful appearance that seemed antithetical to his stature as a scholar.

"Thank you," I said, waiting to hear the punch line.

But there was no punch line. That was pretty much all he said as he flipped through a pile of papers.

I handed him a copy of my most recent paper, a statewide evaluation study using a rigorous control group methodology. This paper showed my strength in conducting field research.

"I hope you don't mind if I just get to the bottom line," I said, launching into a discussion that I hoped would answer the question of when I would be moved to Davis. "I don't know much about decentralization or what it means, but I've heard that my position will be transferred to your department."

"Decentralization is just a political maneuver for improving cost effectiveness of large organizations. Who knows what the real purpose is. For me, I see this as a unique opportunity to expand my department," he said as he waved his arms in the air to signal that he wasn't really interested in politics. He finished by telling me that he considered my position would be an asset.

Describing the faculty members in his department and describing what each did, he added, "You're going to like the relaxed atmosphere and the friendly people here."

He continued, "My department is going to be the best in the world. Better than Berkeley." He paused, grinning sheepishly. I wondered if he knew that I had gone to Berkeley. "I'm expanding the department. We have the office space and are interested in having scientists with new ideas and resources."

"Resources?" I wasn't really clear what he meant.

"Each position at the university is funded. When you arrive here, those funds become part of my departmental resources that can be leveraged to create more resources."

He added, "The funds from your grant will be moved to my department and my administrative staff will provide support for you."

Thinking quickly, I wondered what he meant. The $300,000 grant that I received in 1991 was almost completed and the funds already spent. However, this wasn't the time to discuss details that might derail my whole future!

Changing the subject, I handed Dr. Savage my abbreviated CV, the one I'd prepared to emphasize my academic work. It featured my work at the United Nations Development Programme, where I reviewed nutrition and health field projects.

"I see that you went to Berkeley," Dr. Savage said, flipping through the pages quickly. "Ah . . . your undergraduate work in Biochemistry and Bacteriology . . . graduated with honors . . . hmmm . . . PhD in nutritional sciences," he said, pleasantly looking up at me.

"I guess you'll be moving to Davis." Dr. Savage made a statement but it sounded like a question. I didn't disclose that my spouse of fourteen years wouldn't even discuss the question of our moving to Davis. "No way in bloody hell," was all he said when I tried to talk to him about the fact that my job was moved to Davis and I was forced to either quit or relocate.

Picking up on his interest in "resources," I continued. "I think this move to your department is a wonderful opportunity. I've been exploring an idea for a new kind of funding that would result in hiring a lot of staff."

He looked keenly interested and said, "Go on."

"The new program would be similar to other food and nutrition programs, only this one would feature improving the self-sufficiency of poor families." I wasn't sure if this would sound too much like a welfare program, so I finished quickly. "I'm exploring getting funding from the USDA. And I was hoping to take a sabbatical to get things rolling. I have the opportunity to go to the London School of Hygiene and Tropical Medicine and work with the Human Nutrition Centre there. This would provide the time needed to prepare my proposal."

"Sabbatical?" He thought for a moment. "Good idea. When did you take your last sabbatical?

"I've not had one," I said, trying not to sound annoyed about my past experience in requesting a sabbatical and getting denied.

"Well, I think you should take one. The timing is good. The administrative wheels move slowly; I expect the move might take at least a year, maybe longer. When you return you can give a seminar on your work. What are you proposing?"

Having already requested a sabbatical and having even lined up an institution, this was an easy question to answer. "I've been in communication with Dr. Ericka Wheeler, chair of the Nutrition Centre. They're interested in my providing lectures on American programs aimed at helping poor families. Do you know Dr. Wheeler?"

"Not sure," he answered, and I could see his wheels spinning about my request. "Yes, I think this is a good idea. I'll ask the vice president of agriculture to approve it."

The meeting was suddenly over. I was very relaxed, almost giddy with excitement. This was going to be a really good change for me. Then, without thinking twice, I asked, "Should I write up what we discussed and send it to you for your input?"

As he stood up, he said, "We don't need to put anything in writing." We shook hands, and I wondered if this was a gentleman's agreement. In Oakland, we documented everything.

Later that night, I phoned my husband, Leonard, who was working in Sri Lanka at the time, and he explained the chair's remark to me. "He's telling you not to question a good thing. Just be happy."

The next day I resubmitted my sabbatical proposal, copying the request to Dr. Savage and indicating that I'd met with him and that he was supportive of my taking a sabbatical as soon as possible.

A couple of days later, my request was approved! This was the beginning of something really big, challenging, and worthwhile. My dream of helping poor families in California was soon to be realized. Finally, I was going to be able to do the work I'd been waiting to do—and I was very excited!

We packed our bags and headed off to England, arriving May 1992. My husband, Leonard Joy, a British consultant for the United Nations, was keen on introducing me and our daughter, Judith, now four years old, to his world. We enrolled her in a posh London pre-school called Ravenstone. She was a happy kid who took great joy in the whole "we're-going-to-England" adventure.

At first everything was blissful. Judith looked so cute in her school uniform, and loved the curried lunches and social activities at the school. I met with scholars from around the globe who were debating current poverty issues and politics. Leonard, however, wasn't joining in. He became distant and uncommunicative.

By August 1992, Leonard insisted on returning home. My year-long sabbatical wasn't nearly over, but he threatened to leave me and Judith if we didn't return. So we packed our bags, and after many apologies to my new colleagues in England, Judith and I flew home to be with Leonard. When we got there, he had already made plans to go back to Sri Lanka. I completed my sabbatical at UC Berkeley, finishing the proposal I'd promised my new boss—Dr. Savage.

In April 1993 my sabbatical officially ended. I'd finished the proposal for funding and had begun the process of collecting support and endorsement letters from county organizations who serve the poor. I invited all the university nutrition folks interested in antipoverty programs to join me. I received solid responses from ten colleagues.

I showed Chair Savage the twenty-six endorsement letters and discussed with him my proposal for a nutrition program aimed at improving the health and self-sufficiency of food stamp families in California. The signed letters were from a variety of local, state, and federal agencies: the California Office of Education, the California Housing Authority, food banks, Second Harvest, food pantries, the California Department of Social Services, community action boards, human resource agencies, school principals, as well as county councils of economic opportunity.

My $1.1 million proposal was enthusiastically endorsed by Dr. Savage, who congratulated me for being so proactive. Various UC offices still needed to approve the proposal, and the state agency that manages the food stamp program, and the USDA, who oversees it, had to sign off on the funding.

After I handed a hard copy of the hundred-page proposal to Dr. Savage, he asked me to go with him to the dean's office to talk about my new program. It was now mid-August 1993. My paperwork hadn't yet arrived at Davis, but Dr. Savage assured me that my proposal would be submitted in September under his name.

On our way to the dean's office just before lunch, we strategized on how to promote this million-dollar program. He walked briskly on the dirt path as I tried hard to keep up. The warm August sun was high in the sky, and birds were darting in and out of the creek below us.

"Should I provide him with background?" I asked him as we approached the now bubbling creek.

"Not necessary," he assured me. "If they want to read the proposal, they can do so later." He then explained that he would extol all the virtues of the program and by the time he was done, they would approve it.

"No one is going to say no to a million-plus bucks," he assured me confidently.

That made sense. I was looking down, trying not to trip in my new shoes. I was wearing a light-green dress and cream-colored heels that weren't made for hiking, so I had to keep close watch on the path. I could see a grassy hill in the distance and wondered if my heels would get stuck.

"By the way," Raymond asked me mid-way up the hill, "did you see any of the *Back to the Future* movies?" [2]   He was looking at me intently. I was trying hard to hide the fact that I was already out of breath.

"Ah . . . yeah," I replied quickly without thinking. "Great movie," I added, side-stepping a gopher hole.

"Do you like Michael J. Fox?" he continued. My heart was pounding as I clung to my proposal, which now felt immensely heavy.

'Michael J. Fox?" I repeated trying to make sense of the question. "Oh yes," I said, trying to recall him. "He's a very good actor," I added absentmindedly as the sunlight seared directly into my face. I was beginning to sweat.

"Well, many people have told me that I look like him."

I was taken aback by this statement and tried harder to visualize Michael J. Fox. I wasn't sure how to respond.

I turned to look at Raymond standing in the sun in his khaki shorts, Birkenstocks, and pink polo shirt. Tan and stocky, he looked back at me, his eyes dancing behind wire-rimmed glasses, waiting for my reply. I decided that this wasn't the moment to tell him I wasn't sure.

"Yes, you *do* resemble Michael J. Fox," I fudged.

He beamed. I felt a flush of embarrassment and made a mental note to find out about the movie when I got home.

In the end, our meeting went extraordinary well—I kept my mouth shut while my appreciative boss talked up the proposal with great zeal. I was very gratified when the dean approved it on the spot.

I left work right after the meeting and rushed home. I wanted to tell Leonard all about our meeting with the dean and their approval of my new program.

Len had been working in Sri Lanka for a few years now, going every other month for four to five weeks. I wanted to catch him before he left his hotel room for the day. I went downstairs to Len's office to use his telephone for my call and found a fax in our fax machine.

The fax was for Len. The subject line said, "Arriving today! Eager to see you too!" The fax had been sent by a woman named Clarissa Cross. Clarissa was a designer and artist with whom Len had been consulting about his book—the one he never seemed to finish. He'd often drive across the bay to her Sausalito home for meetings. I had wanted to get to know her, but Len always had some excuse about why she wouldn't be able to come over for dinner.

I'd talked to her on the phone occasionally and even met her once, quite by accident, when I had stopped by a coffee shop in Berkeley on my way to a meeting. They were there having tea together.

I felt a strange sense of anxiety as I read the handwritten fax. Clarissa was confirming her arrival in Sri Lanka. She'd obviously faxed it to the wrong number by mistake. He'd never mentioned to me that she was joining him in Sri Lanka.

In a panic, I looked around at a pile of stuff on his desk and found a folder labeled "C. Cross," which contained all sorts of information. I discovered that she'd been with Leonard in Sri Lanka a year ago. Worse, I found a typed letter that Len had faxed from Sri Lanka to her on Valentine's Day 1992, a few weeks before we'd left to go to England. "Just arrived . . . I am missing you . . . remember the blue boat in the green water? It's still there . . . I think of you . . . and hoping you are making time for us . . . a phone call tonight would be a luxury . . . I am powerfully aware of your spirit . . . I am eager to be with you again . . ."

He'd written the same kind of Valentine stuff to me! My world was about to fall apart.

However, another voice inside me argued that she wasn't the type of woman Len would ever be attracted to. She was so matronly, older, taller, a manly, powerful, mother figure. The image of Leonard's mother that I'd seen in photos of her popped into my head. Nor was this the first time that I suspected him of cheating with Clarissa Cross. That other time, he argued that I was insecure, emotional, jealous, and, probably his best defense at the time, he added, "You have a vivid imagination—Clarissa is a lesbian!"

I phoned the hotel in Sri Lanka, asked for Clarissa Cross, and they rang her room. I was so distraught, I was even prepared to ask her directly about her relationship with my husband.

However, a man, sounding half-asleep, answered and said, "Leonard Joy." Her room was his room! I sunk my teeth into my fist to try to contain myself. Feeling shaky, I said, "Did Clarissa tell you that she sent her fax to the wrong number?" I spoke as casually as I could muster.

"Amy? Is that you?" After a momentary pause, he seemed to wake up. "What's wrong? You're very distant. I can hardly hear you." Len's voice sounded incredibly distressed.

Thinking quickly, I provided all the facts as honestly as I

could. "I read her fax," and concluded with, "I'm not stupid."

He responded, going from pleading to irate. "Wait a minute, what are you suggesting? What fax? How did you know that Clarissa was in Sri Lanka?"

I began a tirade that he quickly put a stop to.

"You're such a suspicious bitch," he screamed, then slammed the phone down.

When we reconnected a couple of days later, I felt a coldness from him I'd never felt before. He had his defenses nicely built up, beginning with, "She's a working colleague; Sri Lanka offered her an assignment; I didn't know she was coming; we're just friends; you jump to conclusions; she's a lesbian," etcetera. I'd heard it all before, had even kind of believed it the first time. He finished by saying that he'd been at the hospital with heart palpitations.

I suddenly felt terribly worried, which made me believe that I still cared about him. As I asked him questions, he started sounding more contrite.

He said the doctor told him he needed to take some medication and visit his own doctor when he returned. At one point, he blamed me for the hospital trip, telling me that the doctor said that I'd stressed him with my hostile phone call. I suggested we start marriage counseling. He sounded reluctant, but I insisted.

I didn't raise the subject of Clarissa again on the telephone. I did communicate that I felt betrayed. In an attempt to soothe my hurt feelings he told me he'd written me a letter, and I'd understand everything after I read it.

The letter arrived a week later, on August 31, 1993. Though I'd decided that I wasn't going to read it right away, curiosity got the better of me.

> My love, the memory of you and being with
> you is still very warm . . . my thoughts of you
> melt and I am just sitting here thinking of you
> . . .No, more than just thinking, I am sensing

you. There are no words to describe how I feel.
What we have is so amazing and inexplicable
... how can I tell you? Do you know how
much I love you? I would never ever do anything that would risk losing you ... in your
heart you know what I say is true ...

He was right: I did feel better after reading it.

Len returned home from Sri Lanka in September. I had
arranged for us to meet with a team, husband and wife marriage
counselors. He'd promised that we'd talk about what happened
in Sri Lanka, although by this time, I had become apprehensive
about discussing it. He was clearly agitated and the mere mention of the counselors sent him into a tizzy. He'd been given
nitroglycerin for chest pain. If I started to talk about Sri Lanka
or even mention Clarissa, he'd reach for the bottle. I postponed
our appointment until I felt he could handle it.

I wondered how on earth I was going to get past this infidel-
ity and move forward with my life. Leonard seemed stuck in
his denial. This wasn't a good sign.

At nine o'clock on a Tuesday morning in September 1993, I
was sitting in the marriage counselor's waiting room. I arrived
early and sat scribbling some quick notes and looking around the
room. One of Monet's water lily paintings hung above a coffee
table with some *New Yorker* magazines.

I opened my purse to make sure I'd brought my copies of
the faxes and letters between Leonard and Clarissa. Leonard
couldn't deny this transgression—I had all the evidence. It was
clear to me that something was going on.

As I sat there waiting, I flashed on the moment I fell in love
with Leonard. I'd bumped into him at the UC's Zellerbach
Hall ticket line in April 1980. This was the same month I began
working at UC Berkeley. He was arguing with the ticket guy,
but all I was hearing was his mesmerizing British accent. Waiting in line for my turn, he walked past, and I said hello. He
told me that he'd forgotten his wallet and they wouldn't hold a

ticket for him. I swooped in and purchased the ticket for him so we could sit together. At the time, I was wildly attracted to him and thought this random encounter was my lucky day.

I recalled his dazzling smile. When he said, "We'll have a smashing good time" his eyes sparkled. Our hands gently touched when I handed him his ticket. I was completely smitten.

Leonard arrived in the waiting room and sat in a chair across from me. I had a hard time looking at him. His hair, now gray and thinning, was neatly combed, and he looked dignified in his tan-colored slacks and shirt. He didn't say a word to me. He flipped through a *New Yorker* magazine and chuckled as he scanned the cartoons.

A tall attractive woman opened the door, introduced herself, and handed me a clipboard with a form to complete. I wondered if she'd be fooled by Leonard. However, when we walked into their counseling room and I met her husband, Gordon, a tall and very powerful-looking man, I relaxed.

"What brings you to see us?" Maxine asked. She had a soothing voice and the tilt of her head conveyed a sense of empathy.

"I made the appointment, so I guess I'll answer the question first," I said professionally, looking directly at Leonard. He seemed slightly amused.

"Go on," Leonard said, still looking amused. Then he laughed.

I'd prepared a short summary of our relationship which I was holding in my hand. I'm thirty, Leonard is fifty-five. We've been together for thirteen years, married for seven of them, with a daughter now four years old. My desire to be diplomatic went out the window when he laughed. Instead, I blurted out what I really wanted to talk about.

"He's cheating on me," I said forcefully.

The room filled with silence. I had hoped that Leonard would say something—but he just sat there. I assumed cheating wasn't big news to marriage counselors so I expected them to jump right in. It was disappointing when they didn't.

"Amy tends to be overly dramatic," Leonard said, his voice resonating great confidence as my hand opened my purse.

I wanted to pull out the fax and pass it around. Instead I changed my mind, put my purse on the floor and used my foot to push it under my chair.

"Leonard travels a great deal," I began. "I discovered that he took a woman on a business trip with him." I paused glancing around the room. No one seemed at all surprised.

"They shared a room," I finally blurted out.

Leonard said nothing.

I expected that they would ask him to explain. They didn't. I started to cry.

Leonard continued to be silent. He even managed to look befuddled by my tears.

"If only he'd open up to me so we can discuss whatever is going on."

Leonard's silence became defiant. I was shocked that he didn't even try to deny the affair. It appeared he didn't even care.

"Leonard," I pleaded, "why did this happen?"

He cleared his voice and simply said, "I'm not having an affair."

He sounded plausible. I suspected that what he said was true. He is not having an affair now. After all, he was caught with his pants down. Appearing to feel nothing, he stifled a yawn.

"I guess Amy has some jealousy issues . . ." he began, letting his voice drop to exude sympathy about my state of mind. His timing was perfect.

Now I was angry. This wasn't going well for me. In fact, I felt on the hot seat.

"Has this feeling of betrayal happened to you before?" Gordon asked trying to diffuse the tension.

"Yes," I said way too quickly, turning my head toward him. I'd forgotten they were even in the room.

Suddenly, I flashed on the night that I discovered that Leonard was romantically involved with two women—one of them was me—and the other was the UC Berkeley provost!

I sat in the chair and felt the urge to tell everything right then and there. I recalled my promise to Doris, my good friend and mentor and the first woman provost at UC Berkeley, who had been Leonard's lover for years. She actually told me all about their breakup, how she had struggled to find and rent an apartment for him in order to get him to move out of her house. It had been a big surprise to her when I told her of my romantic involvement with him many months later. I was young and naïve at twenty-seven—and didn't know that many apparent breakups weren't final. We both got tipsy and giggled that we were sleeping with the same man. Then we swore an oath we'd never tell him our little secret.

"Leonard betrayed me when I found out he was married," I said, avoiding any mention of Doris and our secret. "In 1984 we were about to purchase some property and at the close of escrow the title papers listed him as married."

I looked around to see if Maxine or Gordon registered any surprise. They sat in their chairs completely unmoved. I continued.

"I'd been living with him for four years. He'd never mentioned to me that he didn't bother to get a divorce," I stated as flatly as I could.

I didn't reveal to them or to Leonard that I blamed myself for that incident, because I had simply assumed he was divorced. Of course, the way he spoke about his "first wife" and the fact that he checked the "single" box on his income tax returns was completely consistent with my belief.

"How is this relevant?" Leonard protested. "It's a long story and frankly, water under the bridge," he added with a twinge of annoyance. The clock struck 9:50 a.m.

Although we made another appointment to see them, and we continued with marriage counseling for several years, I could tell this was going to be an uphill battle. Not one to call it quits, I thought it might be helpful to our relationship to persist. I worked hard to try to find a way to forgive him. Years later, he left pages and pages of journal notes for me to read, including an excerpt from December 1993:

> I would like to unburden myself of all that
> I have held in . . . I want to be 100 percent

authentic ... a truly great step would be for
Amy to read my journal ... how else could she
accept me as I am?
   Amy also thinks I have had an affair with
Clarissa. She found my fax ... about meeting
at the airport ... Ah well! Too late, the damage
is done ... everyone does it ... It may be possible to 'be in love' with more than one person
at a time if each reflects some part of one that
one needs to be reflected ..

In April 1994, my move to Davis was officially announced in
the university's newsletter. My first year contract of $1.1 million
was approved on October 28, 1994. Dr. Savage was ecstatic that
his department would be managing this multimillion contract
with the U. S. Department of Agriculture (USDA).

I worked closely with analyst Carolyn Diamond from the
California Department of Social Services (CDSS), and I
admired her honesty, integrity, compassion, and analytical
smarts. She valued my passion for wanting to help the poor. We
formed a unique partnership, publishing a paper together in the
Journal of Nutrition Education about our work in promoting
and improving self-sufficiency in poor populations.

Life in the UC Davis Food, Health and Society Department
was exciting, and many of the people there seemed to share my
interest in helping poor families. Colleagues were friendly and
often invited me to join them for coffee, lunch, or a drink after
work. This was quite different from my experience in Oakland,
where everyone was always rushing to get home. At Davis, I
often stayed late meeting new people and hearing about their
work and families.

I was invited to present my new program at a faculty meeting,
then later as a departmental seminar. Everyone was excited. The
premise of the program was simple: the funds would be used
to hire and train community workers, low-income paraprofessionals to work in poor neighborhoods to improve the life skills

of other struggling families. The educational content was to be practical, focusing on how to plan, shop, and prepare a low-cost and nutritious diet.

The overall programmatic vision was to offer hope for a better future, using nutrition as a step toward promoting self-sufficiency. By hiring community paraprofessionals who themselves were low-income and had empathy for our clients, I was investing in their futures, offering them opportunities to move up in the world.

I believed that these struggling parents wanted their children to have a better life, and that teaching ways to improve their health would be a good first step. This model of "helping people to help themselves" wasn't new, but by using the infrastructure of the university, programs could be implemented in geographical locations across California.

Another goal of our program was to encourage these paraprofessionals to go back to school. Many, mostly bilingual women, did so, and they became professional educators and community leaders. I got to know them well, often sharing photos of our children and stories of our lives. We were all connected by a desire for our children to have a better life and by a passion for helping others do the same. When making presentations to local boards of supervisors or at formal hearings, I'd bring one of them to share her own firsthand experience.

Years before, when I interviewed then congressman Leon Panetta, chair of the House Budget Committee, and published a paper with his comments, he referred to our work as "an investment in the future." [3] To me, this was the best job in the world. I loved knowing that at the end of the day, I was proud of our goals and our accomplishments.

The stage was now set, and my boss and biggest fan, Dr. Raymond Savage, was cheering me on.

3 | Beverly

In November 1994, I hired the recently retired assistant VP, Gloria Jones, to assist me in setting up the program at UC Davis. Gloria was doing a lot of consulting on program development and had a great reputation for getting things done.

Five months later, Gloria interviewed a very charming and flamboyant administrative assistant named Beverly Benford, who appeared to have a range of useful skills and a background to match.

"You're going to be impressed with Beverly," Gloria told me as she signed off on the paperwork. "She has a master's degree in public administration and has even taught classes here at Davis," she buzzed excitedly.

"And, by the way, she has a friend in high places rooting for her," Gloria added, mentioning someone I didn't know in the dean's office.

I met Beverly on May 1, 1995, her first day of work. She was polished, professional, and organized. She was also highly motivated to advance herself professionally.

"Nice to meet you," Beverly said to me with a friendly smile as she warmly took my hand to shake it. She was dressed in a professional yet elegant black dress with a tailored cream jacket. "I've heard about your work on reducing poverty in California," Beverly continued, "and this is what I want to do. I want to help poor families."

"Call me Amy," I said, looking her in the eye. She had done her homework and caught what others always missed: that my goal was to help poor families.

I noted her firm handshake. As I let go, I also saw a flash of sadness in her eyes that took me by surprise and made me wonder if poverty had a deeper meaning for Beverly.

Beverly turned her head away, as though she had revealed too much. That flash of sorrow would haunt me for a very long time.

For the next eighteen months, Beverly was trained by Gloria to take over many administrative and personnel functions. Budgetary matters were handled at the department level. Within two years, Beverly had worked her way up in the organization, getting to know everyone and making sure everyone knew her. And for the next decade, Beverly and I worked shoulder to shoulder. She became my ally and friend, someone I trusted and cared for.

"Good afternoon ladies and gentleman, welcome to our first statewide conference. My name is Amy Block Joy, and I'm the director. As you know, we've come together to begin the process of building a program to help reduce poverty in California. The mission of our program is to improve the health and well-being of low-income families throughout the state."

I was speaking at the Clarion Hotel at the San Francisco Airport to about 150 university employees and others interested in reducing poverty. It was the summer of 1997. I believed this two-day event to celebrate our fourth-year achievements would help staff share ideas, learn from one another, discover new teaching methods, and work together to build the future. I wanted the group to feel enthusiastic about the job ahead. Everyone in the room shared my passion for helping poor families.

To make sure that everyone felt involved, I had convened a planning committee to work on the conference arrangements, speakers, educational activities, and food. As event coordinator, Beverly did a superb job in getting a very reasonable price at the Clarion Hotel and arranging all the logistics, including meals, break-out rooms, and program materials. I was impressed. My previous experience on conference planning included firsthand knowledge of how easily people can get bent out of shape. For some it was the food; others found the hotel uncomfortable; many complained about the speakers, the traffic, and the weather.

Beverly and I brainstormed about all possible scenarios with the committee. We planned ways to excite the staff, including jazzy name tags and conference canvas bags. We developed a stimulating program that included a variety of speakers, activities to get people moving around the room to meet each other, and a number of sharing sessions. We developed a fun nutrition quiz with small educational incentives, including inexpensive cooking timers, magnets for the refrigerator, measuring cups, and brightly colored cooking aprons. All items included a printed nutrition message.

I wanted our staff filled with anticipation and excitement.

When I arrived the night before, I was greeted as a dignitary. Beverly had hinted to me for a whole week that there was a surprise in store for me. I was so busy that I completely forgot what she'd told me and when the bellhop took me up to my room, I was sure he'd taken me to the wrong place.

Beverly had booked me a deluxe suite with a large conference room, a kitchen with a bar, and a large-screen TV. I told the bellhop that he'd made a mistake, so he called down to the lobby. The desk clerk told me the room was free due to the number of guests, mentioning Beverly as the contact person who'd made the arrangements.

I declined the suite and asked to be moved to a regular room and told the hotel that they had to put my room costs on the bill. Suites were often offered, but as a university employee I was required to decline such offers, which were considered gifts. When I met with Beverly over dinner, she was quite gracious about my having turned down the room and even winked at me to indicate that she also was a stickler for following university rules.

"Great minds think alike," was her comment when I reminded her that university policy didn't allow for freebies. She promised to get the master bill sorted out in the morning.

"Beverly, I know you wanted to surprise me and probably

thought I'd enjoy the luxury," I began as we were mulling over the dinner choices. She interrupted.

"Your surprise wasn't the room!" she protested. "The surprise was a special dessert in your honor at tomorrow's big lunch. Look, it's here on the menu." She pointed to the "double bitter-sweet chocolate fudge cake with a scoop of homemade vanilla ice cream," then stopped while I stared dumbfounded at the menu.

"You want to order it right now, don't you?" she asked, teasingly. I couldn't believe that she hadn't caught on to what my real reaction was about. I'd be roasted on the spit for such hypocrisy: we tell people to reduce their fat intake, then order chocolate cake for their dessert!

"Beverly," I began, wondering how she'd take my decision. "Yes, I'll order the cake for dessert tonight, and will definitely enjoy it," I said returning her smile. "But our staff will have a coronary if there's cake served for dessert at the big lunch tomorrow. I'm sorry, but we're going to have to change the dessert order to fruit," I said, noting big disappointment in Beverly's face.

"Maybe the hotel can find some kind of interesting flavored sorbet to go with the fruit?" I offered by way of appeasement.

Beverly brightened. I wrote it down on the pad that I always carried with me and handed her the piece of paper so she'd not forget.

After dinner, I ordered the cake for dessert. We both joked about what might have been written on the conference evaluation if this cake had been served. I thought that probably everyone would eat it and secretly enjoy it, but in the end I would be severely criticized for violating our nutrition motto.

"Director Joy screwed up big time," I said, pretending to quote an evaluation while scooping up the delicious cake that was headed for my open mouth. "Let them eat cake, wasn't one of her brightest ideas." I finished my sentence just before savoring the heavenly mixture of chocolate and vanilla.

The next day she told me that the dessert had been changed and that the hotel would charge me for my room on the master bill.

Martin Yan of the *Yan Can Cook* show on the local public television station agreed to do a cooking demonstration for our program staff and charge only a small fee to cover travel and expenses. His demonstration was thrilling, allowing many of the staff to help him as he worked the room. His book, *Martin Yan's Culinary Journey Through China*, sold like hotcakes.[4]

Chef Yan also provided an inspirational message about cooking and food, and the value of artful presentations. We instituted the cooking demonstration as a solid teaching tool to get people to improve their diet. Because many of the people we enrolled in the program lacked cooking skills, introducing them back into the kitchen was a major step toward improving their diet, getting children and parents to eat together, and showing that healthy food can look and taste good, and be inexpensive and fun to prepare.

By the year 2000, Beverly was managing a bustling office. She took financial, personnel, and management classes, and continued to provide excellent results, working late at night and becoming an effective administrator. She'd also, by this time, established herself as very popular with those in charge.

"I'll be right back," Beverly would tell me whenever I would see her in the mail room making copies and chatting with some of my colleagues. When she returned, she'd have some interesting tidbits of news about someone.

"Guess who wants me to review a job description?" she would brag, adding that the department's human resource manager asked her to participate in some high-level interviews. I was pleased that she was so much a part of the Food, Health and Society Department family and that others appreciated her as much as I did.

Beverly also seemed to "get me." She had an uncanny knack for knowing exactly what I wanted and where I was headed. One day, after I shared a story about my Jewish grandmother, Celia Levy, Beverly told me she was Jewish and that her mother's maiden name was also Levy. I registered surprise because I had thought Beverly was Jamaican. I asked her about Jamaica, but Beverly looked teary-eyed and said that she didn't want to talk about it. I had no idea about the Jewish population in Jamaica, so I didn't press her nor did I question that she was telling the truth.

Beverly found other ways to make me feel that we had a special connection. For instance, she began using the same corny expressions I used. I felt flattered when she'd say, "We're on the same page," or "Great minds think alike," or "I value your contributions." I began to feel that I finally had found someone who really understood and appreciated me.

Unlike Len, she behaved as though she not only understood what was needed but was two steps ahead of me. If someone was angry at me, Beverly might suggest that they're having a bad day. I'd especially feel bad if another woman was angry at me, thinking, we're woman and we're struggling for the same things. With Beverly, I felt validated. She appeared to be kind-hearted, even compassionate, often commenting that she was proud of all the work we'd accomplished for poor families.

I remember one occasion when someone wanted me to approve their out-of-state travel to attend a nutrition conference. I'd sent an email to the individual denying their request and explaining that our funds were earmarked for in-state travel only. I'd worded the email very carefully so as not to ruffle any feathers. The next day, I read her very curt, frankly angry response. The woman even wrote that she'd heard that I approved someone else to travel to the same conference, implying that I was treating her unfairly. I explained in another matter-of-fact email that I hadn't approved out-of-state travel for anyone.

When I went to tell Beverly this saga, she came immediately to my defense. "You're too nice for these people. They don't appreciate you!" and I found my eyes getting teary. I wasn't even aware how hurt I was feeling most of the time; as a director in charge of a lot of money, I'd long ago accepted the fact that people were going to be pushy and demanding. Beverly even recited by verse exactly the policy forbidding out-of-state travel. Then she found the page in the federal guidelines where the policy was explicitly stated and marked the page with a post-it. Together we decided to develop a list of what is and is not allowed when using federal funds so everyone would understand that the rules would be enforced equally and fairly.

I was very impressed by Beverly's ability to quickly grasp what was needed. What I didn't know until several years later was that she had the password to my computer and was reading all my emails.

That same year, 2001, I found numerous clues to what Leonard had in mind for my future. His mood swings became more difficult to handle, and he threatened to leave. When he began leaving little notes in the kitchen indicating that he was looking for an apartment, I became concerned that he'd bolt. During a session with a marriage counselor, Leonard produced divorce papers. The amount of alimony I would have to pay him was terrifying.

The alimony calculator, a benign-looking "DissoMaster," was a software program used by divorce attorneys to compute alimony for the spouse most in-need. Salary and other sources of income were the major determinates of the alimony calculation, and Leonard's attorney had used my correct salary. However, Leonard's only income as shown in this DissoMaster printout was "unemployment benefits." The result was that Leonard would be entitled to half my income for a very long time, perhaps even permanently. Unless Leonard had solid employment, which seemed unlikely, Judith and I would be destitute. I consulted a divorce attorney who advised me to hold off until Leonard found employment or a new life partner. A second opinion by another attorney agreed. This wasn't my most dignified decision, but it was one I felt I could live with until Judith was safely in college.

The program continued to be quite successful and by 2003 had reached an annual budget of $14 million. I created a grant program to increase faculty involvement. Beverly provided budgetary assistance, and her popularity increased dramatically. My boss, Dr. Savage, was a big fan of hers.

Often Beverly and I would meet with him in his corner office on the third floor to provide updates on the program. He was mostly interested in what he called the "budget numbers." He often asked me to make presentations at faculty meetings. Beverly would remind me that he was really impressed with my work, and it wasn't long before he began to openly praise Beverly.

"I'm impressed with the program's growth," Dr. Savage said to us during a meeting in April 2003. "Can you make a graph of the increase in funding over the past five years?"

I nodded. "I already prepared a graph on program growth and cost effectiveness for the USDA," I said proudly.

Beverly piped in. "I could add our new budget numbers to the graph. The amount of funding has doubled," she added excitedly.

"Excellent," Dr. Savage said, looking appreciatively at Beverly. "Can you revise Amy's graph—I just need the budget numbers," he added.

"When do you need it?" Beverly asked jumping to attention.

"Now," Dr. Savage said and stood up, talking only to Beverly. She hustled out the door.

"Are there other charts or graphs we can prepare for you?" I asked, picking up my briefcase.

"Let Beverly do it," Dr. Savage answered rubbing his hands together. "She knows exactly what I need."

By 2004, the program had been in operation for ten years, and I had brought over $80 million in federal money to the university. My meetings with Dr. Savage and Beverly were fairly routine, although over time they became less frequent. One time, after she gave me a pep talk about how other faculty members were envious of my success, she quoted Raymond many times. I was struck that she was calling him Raymond, and I asked her why she was meeting with him. Her demeanor radically changed.

"Oh, did I say I met with him? I meant that I bumped into

him in the hallway. We spoke in the hallway."

I received my three-year promotions as required to maintain my academic standing. The university had stopped giving cost-of-living raises, so the only way to receive a raise was through an increase in rank, called a promotion, or "rank step increase." More significantly, I worked like a dog to get things done. Dr. Savage, or Raymond as I also now began to call him, continued to be very friendly, showering me with appreciation and recognition.

Beverly frequently let me know that she was working day and night. If I needed background information, she'd do all the work for me. She retrieved items from the files and prepared complex budget reports. She catered to my every professional need and my workaholic tendencies.

"You don't have time to find things in the files. You're the director, let me get it," she'd say to me. She'd scoot me back to my office, happily offering to drop everything to help me. "I know where that report is," she'd tell me, running off to find it. And she'd find it, quickly and promptly.

In July 2004, my colleagues started putting pressure on me to apply for more money for the 2005 contract. Many colleagues were failing to get grants as funding sources literally dried up and those available became highly competitive. Nevertheless, many believed my contract money was readily available.

The fact was, as the program grew, the contract approval process got harder and harder. Our program was teaching more than 110,000 food stamp clients in forty-two counties of California. I was worried that more money meant more paperwork, and we were already maxed out in that department. Although I knew that a certain amount was necessary, I worried that too many bureaucratic demands would reduce creativity. I walked a very fine line, making sure that the program staff were following the rules, yet allowing my creative colleagues some latitude for inspiration. However, many were critical of my attempts to keep the program at a capped funding level. Some Davis academic folks began thinking of this money as some kind of magic bullet and considered me too rigid, too strict, and too short-sighted. It was Beverly who told me what Raymond had said.

"Raymond asked me to set up a meeting with you, Darci, and himself to talk about increasing the budget," Beverly told me.

"Increasing it?" I asked.

"Look, Amy," she began assertively, "Raymond has heard that you are holding the purse strings too tightly. He said that people are complaining."

I didn't have the time or inclination to argue with either Beverly or Raymond. If we wanted to get more money, we needed folks to do the work that had been promised after a USDA review. The deadline for adding new programs had already passed.

"I've already set up the meeting for Monday," Beverly said firmly. "Remember, he's the chair of the department." It would be stupid for me to not go along with what Beverly was suggesting, although the increase would never be approved because the deadline had passed.

Early in 2004, Beverly seemed to be running out of steam and started becoming moody and tense. Something was out of whack. She had begun to behave more erratically, arguing and getting into spats with office staff and others. I discussed my concerns with Raymond, and he assured me that Beverly was fine. He said, "You worry too much, my friend. Everyone has a bad day now and then. Relax. Go smell the flowers."

Things heated up when Beverly managed to get into a fight with Joanne Willow, a university program analyst who'd been with the university for thirty years. She worked in another program in our department, in a position of a similar rank to Beverly's. The nasty fight between them was about a plastic grape plant that had been moved and a broken branch was found on the floor. Beverly had purchased the plant and was enraged that it had been damaged and shoved aside. Joanne quoted "office safety" as a reason for moving it, claiming that a large plastic plant shouldn't be placed near a toaster oven because it might start a fire.

I wasn't in the office that day in August 2004. After several

years of daily commuting, I'd started telecommuting, going up
to Davis three days a week.

The chair was out of the country, so I went up to Davis to
meet with Beverly face-to-face and consult with Dr. Fred Stone,
the vice-chair. As is often the case, both parties were wrong.
The incident, however, had escalated rather bizarrely. The plastic plant wasn't truly a fire hazard, and Beverly had overreacted
by yelling at Joanne and then widely distributing an accusatory
and derogatory email about the incident. Several of the department folks took Beverly's side, claiming that she was in charge
of room renovations.

I resolved the incident by helping Beverly send a written
apology to Joanne. Beverly's letter was accepted by Fred Stone.
Raymond sent me a congratulatory email for my efforts.

When Raymond returned the following week from his trip
overseas, I met with him and learned that it was he who had
originally invited Beverly to chair the office renovation committee. I laughed and reminded him that this "expensive plant"
was fake. To me the whole thing was ridiculous.

He didn't laugh; in fact, he appeared angry and made some
comments about how people were calling him and complaining about my rigid interpretation of the program guidelines.
At the time, his comment seemed strangely out of place, and I
chalked it up to a "bad mood," but it stuck with me. I wondered
about this committee. When I asked Beverly she said that she
had a friend who gave the department a good quote on office
furniture. I began to worry that her influence was getting out
of hand.

A week later, I met with Raymond again and asked him
directly who was complaining about me. He was vague and said,
"Don't worry. Everyone is envious about the amount of money
you have. People complain because they feel you're hoarding it,
and they want their share. People can be really nasty and devi-
ous." Just when I thought he was done, he added, "And they
want Beverly to work for them, not you. She's very popular. You
have a great person working for you—never forget that. She's

essential to your work."

I felt that he implied that she was popular and I wasn't. I began to wonder about their relationship. I met with Beverly to discuss my concerns about the plastic plant incident. She made a comment about Joanne, even suggesting that Joanne had been going around the department saying negative things about me. I was floored. I told Beverly that I wasn't interested in any more office gossip.

Besides these minor incidents, we secured almost $14 million of funding for the following year.

The following summer of 2005, I had still not completely forgotten Beverly's gossip and the chair's veiled accusations against me. Then in August, I hosted a small private baby shower for Beverly's son and daughter-in-law in our office. I discovered that Beverly had invited several of my department colleagues. She carried on as though they were her exclusive best buddies. Watching her laughing with them over the punch bowl, I wondered if I'd missed something. Indeed, after I met Rebecca, one of Beverly's short-term temps still employed four years later, I wondered—*how come I've never met her before?*

However, the biggest surprise was meeting Beverly's mother. She was obviously not Jewish, and I began to have doubts. Why would someone lie about being Jewish?

Although perplexed, my mind was preoccupied by an upcoming national conference in Washington DC. Beverly was going to meet me there after going to Florida on a weekend vacation.

Several disturbing events took place during early September 2005. Beverly left for Florida three days early, telling me that Raymond had approved her new departure date while I was away from the office. Next, Beverly was a "no-show" at the DC conference; and most significantly, neither Beverly nor Raymond replied to any of my many urgent emails, voicemails, or phone calls asking what happened.

There was no excuse for not returning any of my messages as

we all had working Blackberries.

I became quite alarmed when I arrived in DC on September 10 and was told at the front desk that Beverly had cancelled her reservation. Initially I was concerned about her, wondering if she'd had some sort of emergency. But my Blackberry remained silent for three days until the chair communicated that he wanted to meet with me.

"We need to talk," was all he wrote.

When I returned on Wednesday, September 14, I heard that one of Beverly's staff, Tessa Romanoski, administrative assistant and purchaser for my office, had met with the chair then promptly resigned. I was annoyed that I hadn't been briefed by Beverly, who was, for some unknown reason, refusing to talk to me. I scheduled a phone call with Raymond to discuss my concerns.

At two in the afternoon exactly I dialed his number and he answered. He told me he was leaving for South Africa the next day, and there were some things we needed to sort out. He sounded irritated.

"The overall mood in your office is very bad," he said "We can't keep having this tension between you and Beverly. I've told you before she's under a lot of pressure, and you've got to give her some slack."

Taken aback by his statement, I told him I was concerned about Beverly, specifically her lack of communication with me, and asked him, rather forcefully, what had happened last week. He avoided answering directly, instead reminding me over and over again that Beverly was stressed. I persisted.

"What about Tessa? Did she and Beverly have some sort of incident?"

There was more silence on his end, but I waited. "Oh, yes, Tessa, yes, she resigned." He was now stuttering and raising his voice.

"Your office is falling apart. She's the second of your employees who came to see me, threatening to resign. I managed to talk the other one out of leaving. Don't ask me who it is—it's enough for you to know that she's not happy. You simply need to tread more lightly." His voice was very gruff as he continued.

"This is larger than just Beverly. A significant number of individuals, at multiple levels, are concerned about you. I've had to tell folks that you're under a lot of stress due to problems with your grant."

I said nothing, biting my lip. *Why is he attacking me,* I wondered. I wanted to give him a piece of my mind, after all I was the director. There weren't any problems with the funding—we'd already gotten approval for the next year.

"The program is fine. It's Beverly that I'm concerned about," I said, steaming with indignation.

He then relaxed a little. "You need to get a grip on things, my friend. This has been an exceptionally difficult time."

His use of the "my friend" was the clue that he'd softened. Also backing down, I stopped firing questions at him. I'd almost forgotten that he was my supervisor and the head of the department.

"Tessa's resignation makes no sense to me. I'm perplexed." I didn't reveal to him that I'd already asked everyone I knew why she resigned, and they all steered me back to Beverly, who was completely avoiding me.

"Let's talk about it when I get back from South Africa. For now, don't talk to anyone, and I mean no one. Especially, stay away from Beverly. I mean it. If we lose her, everything will fall apart."

"Fall apart . . . I'm not understanding you now."

"You're working too hard. It's getting to the point of no return. I'm concerned that Beverly will leave. We have to stop all the bickering." He stopped and waited for my response.

"What do you suggest?" I asked.

"First, you need to keep away from Beverly. She's quite upset. You need a break from all this. We can talk more when I return from my trip."

Stunned, I began to try to piece together the puzzle. Something has happened while I was in DC. *Is Raymond protecting Beverly?*

Raymond approved a four-month sabbatical for me, beginning September 15. That was the day he took over the supervision of Beverly. I happily agreed since I did want to publish a paper for the program and was invited by a news journalist to work on a television show for KVIE, a local PBS station on a nutrition program for children.

However, avoiding contact with Beverly wasn't really an option, and I wanted to find out what happened with Tessa.

"Bev, what happened with Tessa?" I asked two months later, my eyes pleading for the truth. I had taken Beverly out to celebrate her December birthday at a local fancy restaurant. Beverly lifted her chin as she forcefully dropped her steaming cup of tea. I saw a flash of rage in her eyes as the cup rattled in the saucer.

Months later, she continued her refusal to say anything about Tessa's departure until I eventually gave up and stopped asking. I couldn't help noticing that Beverly was very distracted, worried, and unbelievably cold.

How could I have not seen what was staring me right in the face?

It was early February 2006. I was meeting with Beverly in my office and asked to see a report. She yawned and said she'd get it later from the files.

I got up from my chair and said, "Let's go get it now."

We were sitting face-to-face, I in my desk chair and Beverly seated in a chair near my closed door. She became visibly tense and started rapidly clicking the ballpoint pen she was holding.

"If you insist, I'll get it for you," Beverly said harshly. She wouldn't look at me. I'd done nothing to spark her change in demeanor.

"I'll go with you," I said cheerfully, getting up from my chair.

"Sit down," Beverly said to me, her voice tense.

I stared at her, surprised, and remained standing.

And then, out of the blue, she began speaking rapidly in a high-pitched voice. "You need to hear what people are saying about you," Beverly began. "You have no idea. They've gone to the chair again to complain . . ." I knew I didn't want to hear any more gossip.

"I really need that file and I need it now," I said, interrupting her.

I walked quickly to the door.

Beverly began yelling. "Just because you're the director doesn't give you the right to yell at me. I'm going to report you to Raymond. You know, he and I have a very good relationship . . . very close . . . we're like this!" She was holding up her two fingers, tightly entwined, and wagged them at me.

Feeling disconcerted at how quickly her mood had shifted, I opened the door and said, "Beverly, you need to go back to your office and cool off. We can resume our meeting later when you feel better."

I repeated my request for her to leave my office as I stepped into the hallway.

She stormed out, stomping her feet. Everyone in the office next door could hear what was going on, and they looked down when she entered their room. She was grumbling and sounded like she might explode.

About ten minutes later, she sent an email to me requesting permission to leave for the day because she wasn't feeling well. The wording was professional, and I was greatly relieved. I replied quickly with my approval, and added that we'd resume our discussion after she'd had some time to think about what was troubling her.

After she left, I went to the files located in the room next to her office. They were all locked and I didn't have a key.

The next day, still feeling a bit wary after what had happened the day before, I asked Beverly about the locked files. She provided an explanation that was reasonable and made sense.

"This is a federal program. We have to keep the information confidential, and I don't trust people taking things out of the files and then not returning them."

She even followed up with an email alerting everyone that they needed to ask her approval to use the files because some had gone missing. She quoted a federal guideline about the importance of confidentiality. At the end of her email she reminded everyone that I was the director of the program.

Later the same day, I asked for the key to the files. She showed me where the key was kept and said that all the drawers were left open during the work day. I went to find a project report and removed it from the drawer. On my way back to my office, she stopped me to see what I'd taken, making a copy for me and putting the original back in the drawer that I'd left open.

The next day I reviewed the report Beverly had copied for me. I found what I thought was an error in one of her budget sheets. My project's budget had been increased by $150,000, and a notation stated that the funds were for Dr. Savage. I sent Raymond a confidential letter reporting this "budget irregularity" and urgently requested a meeting.

Instead of offering a meeting time, he responded to my email with a terse "Your letter is fine." It seemed he hadn't even read it. I went up to his office the same day, February 27, 2006, determined to get to the bottom of this.

I didn't have an appointment, but his door was open so I walked in.

"Raymond, there seems to be a mistake, a $150,000 mistake!" I began nervously, sitting down on the couch by the door.

"Let's see." He reached over as I handed him a copy of the budget. I'd highlighted the figure in yellow. I'd circled all the relevant details, the additional $150,000, and his name next to the figure.

"Oh, it's just a math error. Ask Beverly to correct it. Anything else?" he asked, handing me back both copies.

"But Raymond, don't you think this is a rather large amount to be an error?" I was puzzled that he seemed so nonchalant.

"Happens all the time. No big deal. Easy to correct." And he stood up, indicating the meeting was over.

I asked Beverly to correct the budget. She appeared embarrassed, blamed Rebecca for the math error, apologized, and said she'd take care of it right away. She was appropriately contrite. I told Raymond about her response, and he replied with one word, "Excellent."

Unsatisfied and more determined than ever to get to the bottom of this, I returned to the files that very afternoon. I sat down and went through all the files that were related to Dr. Savage. Beverly kept coming over to ask if she could help.

"Thanks. You've organized the files very well. It's easy to find things," I said cheerfully. She was clearly agitated.

In fact, Beverly had made it easy for me to find all the files for Chair Raymond Savage. Even with thousands of files in the many drawers in the office, she'd put all of Raymond's information under one word: EQUINOX.[5] The chair had signed a multimillion dollar contract with the EQUINOX Food Company, makers of a whole line of popular and expensive healthy food products, including high fiber fruit bars, frozen vegetarian entrees, a variety of international condiments enriched with supplements, and fancy low-calorie desserts. Discreetly pulling the file out of the drawer to look through it, I wondered why a file marked EQUINOX was in our office.

It didn't take me long to find something truly odd. Tucked neatly away in this folder containing twenty old invoices and letters, I pulled out a purchase order that knocked my socks off! It was an invoice marked "paid" for a Canon Optura 600 costing $1,400.74 from Fry's Electronics. My signature wasn't on it.

What is a Canon Optura 600? How did this get purchased? This time I decided not to consult with Raymond. Instead, I called Fry's Electronics, a store in Sacramento that sold computers, TV set, stereos, and other goods.

Mystified, I couldn't help but wonder, *What on earth is Raymond doing?*

4 | Enough!

I called Fry's Electronics on Tuesday, February 28, 2006, and asked for Dave, whose phone number was on the purchase order. The woman who answered put me on hold. Staring closely at the purchase order I'd found in the files the day before, I thought about what I was going to say to Dave.

It looked routine, except that I hadn't approved it. What also caught my eye was that the item was quite pricy, especially given the lack of information about it.

"Canon Optura 600" was all that was written in the large space for item description. The cost was way over the amount we usually spent on program supplies. We never purchased items over five hundred dollars except computers, which we always purchased through the university vendor, Dell Computer. This particular store, Fry's Electronics, was virtually unknown to me except for its annoying TV commercial. *Your best buys are always at Fry's. Guaranteed!!*

When Dave came to the phone I had already decided to simply ask him about the item.

"Hi, Dave. I have a quick question for you. What's a Canon Optura 600?" I gave him the item number and he said he'd look it up.

A few minutes later he said, "Got it. The Canon Optura is a DVD camcorder," Dave told me.

I was more than a little surprised. "Why is a DVD player so expensive?" I asked.

"It's a camcorder," he repeated the word. "Camcorders make

DVDs. I suppose it also plays them. But this one is very small, a mini-DVD camcorder. You can hold it in the palm of your hand. The price includes computer software, a 200X digital zoom, special filters, high resolution imagery, carrying case, and hard drive accessories." He added, "Most people use their computer to edit and play the DVD."

"Thanks Dave. You've been very helpful," and I hung up.

We don't buy camcorders for our program because we don't make our own DVDs; we buy professionally produced educational DVDs for teaching purposes. Obviously, this purchase wasn't for the program, so this would have to be considered misuse of funds. Ouch! Something had to be done and quickly.

Why would anyone take such a risk? I asked myself while I was waiting for the elevator. *Did they think they'd get away with it? Whatever's going on, it's gotta stop. How serious is this? What are the consequences?* Over the next few days, I thought about these questions a million times.

But first, I had to be sure I'd uncovered the truth.

"Have you been waiting long?" Beverly said as she walked toward me from the hallway leading to the elevator.

Leaning on the wall next to the elevator, I turned to look at Beverly, who at sixty-four looked robust and confident. A decade older than I, she seemed upbeat. My laid-back style was now about to be tested. *Am I up to this? Can I do it?*

A small pink notepad in her right hand, Beverly paced in front of the elevator. She carried her heavy frame with a fair amount of gracefulness.

I nodded a quick hello, moving my briefcase to my other hand so she could stand next to me. We were riding up to the third floor together to meet with Raymond. I usually took the stairs, but Beverly always took the elevator, and I wanted to go up with her. This was going to be an important meeting.

"What are you doing over the weekend?" I asked to fill the gap as we waited for the elevator doors to open. I was expecting our meeting to be difficult, and I didn't want her to notice that I was nervous.

"Oh, not much . . ." Beverly murmured as the elevator doors opened.

"Cool sweater. Is it new?"

"Yes, as a matter of fact!" Beverly said, twirling around to show it off. She was wearing a jazzy dark purple knitted button-down sweater with large, glitzy rhinestone buttons, which accented her full figure. As usual, I was dressed in my Jones of New York conservative gray business suit.

"It looks good on you." Then, changing the subject, I asked as the elevator lurched when the doors closed, "Did you make enough copies of the preliminary budget for Raymond?"

"Yep!" Beverly replied in her usual curt and confident manner. "He's going to lick his lips over next year's budget," she said, almost giddy with excitement. "We're almost to $15 million." She proudly handed me the copies of her budget report and I opened my briefcase and put them in. *Oh Bev,* I sighed to myself.

I momentarily flashed on the lunch with Beverly a year ago when her eyes sparkled as she declared, "You're the best boss ever!" Memories of Beverly flooded me as I thought about our elbow-to-elbow partnership. She was my work buddy who was constantly reminding me of her loyal support, telling others that she was my one-woman fan club. She really knew and appreciated me, consoling me during stressful times. We celebrated birthdays, not to mention all the accomplishments and success stories of our work together. I recalled Beverly's more personal side that would bubble to the surface when she shared her most intimate secrets. The million coffee breaks and happy events that connected us, including my daughter's Bat Mitzvah and her son's wedding.

I fondly recalled the day she insisted on taking me out for a "do I have something to tell you!" hot fudge sundae. These memories stuck in my throat as I stood next to her in the elevator.

"Are you okay?" Beverly asked looking at me quizzically.

"I'm fine, why?" I answered clutching my briefcase tightly.

"I don't know. You look tense."

I felt very close to tears and the thought of what I was about to do sickened me.

I loved my job. It had taken twenty-six years for me to get to where I was. The actual work was challenging, even frustrating, but at the end of the day, I felt fulfilled. I reflected again on my dilemma. I couldn't predict what would happen next. Yet, this was serious and couldn't wait. *I'm done with soul searching,* I thought. I was now prepared for the fight of my life.

The elevator bell rang announcing our arrival on the third floor.

I held the elevator doors open for Beverly, then followed her out. Leaving the elevator, I tripped and the papers in my briefcase spilled all over the floor. I worried my nervousness was now showing.

Beverly whirled around in surprise. I wasn't usually clumsy. "Are you sure you're okay?" she asked, bending down to help me collect the papers.

For a second, I froze, wondering if Beverly had noticed anything.

"If you're nervous about discussing the budget in front of Raymond, don't worry, I'll do all the talking," Beverly assured me. "He never questions me."

I thought to myself, *Funny you should say that, Raymond is always questioning me.*

We arrived a little early and sat outside his closed office door. I thought about Raymond, and I wondered how he'd respond. *Do I really know him? What really goes on behind his closed door?*

I recalled our first meeting twelve years before, and my admiration of him at the time. It seemed so long ago, those days when I'd idealized him as if he were some kind of superstar.

Raymond was now approaching middle age. He still had a youthful get-up-and-go appearance, with his tawny-brown wavy hair, wire-rimmed glasses, and surfer build. I appreciated his intelligence and work ethic. He valued my contributions to helping poor families, frequently sending me short, enthusiastic emails that conveyed his appreciation. He'd reply to my frequent updates with praise, even suggesting we should celebrate my success with champagne.

He became chair fifteen years before, and many referred to him as the "wonder boy" of the university. He was a powerful man and pretty much unstoppable when it came to building up his department.

Sitting in the chair outside his office, I recalled our first meeting and how he called me an "asset." Since then, I'd attended almost all of his faculty meetings, sitting next to him and watching how he managed each meeting. Smoothly efficient in getting through his agenda, he was calm, professionally cool, and clearly in charge.

When I first arrived in the department, he had the reputation of going from office to office collecting "votes" on departmental matters. What he was doing was highly political. He wanted to be sure to get what he wanted and was very persuasive. During meetings, he'd report the voting results and no one dared to contradict him. But now I was going up against him. His assistant was not at her desk, and his office door had a sign that said, "Please knock."

At exactly two o'clock, I stood up and said to Beverly, "Are you ready?"

Repeating silently to myself, *I can do this, I can do this,* I looked at Beverly and then at the clock. My mouth was very dry and I wondered if I should get a bottle of water. I'd pressed my leg so hard against the chair while waiting, it had fallen asleep, and I had difficulty standing up. I shifted my weight so my foot could wake up.

I knocked. We heard his voice say, "Come in."

I opened the door, took a deep breath, and followed Beverly into Raymond's office.

He was sitting at his computer and turned around when we walked in. He was wearing khaki shorts, a brightly colored Hawaiian shirt, and his usual Birkenstocks. He motioned for us to sit.

I shut the door quietly. I motioned for Beverly to take the

couch next to the door and I pulled over one of his chairs, positioning it so I could see both their faces during the meeting. Raymond pushed his swivel chair away from his desk and inched toward us.

I pulled out three copies of my two-page letter. Beverly, of course, believed I was pulling out her budget report.

"I have something that I need to discuss—a confidential matter, something very serious."

I handed a copy of the letter to each of them. My voice was shrill, and I felt a little shaky with a stomach full of butterflies.

Beverly looked at me puzzled.

Raymond's posture changed. He'd been slumped in his chair looking bored, and now he sat upright and at attention in his very big chair. Beverly sucked in some air and although she didn't cough out loud, she started blinking fast, as though both surprised and disoriented.

"This is a confidential letter about a difficult subject, and I thought it'd be best for me to read it out loud while you two followed along with your printed copies."

My hands trembled as I began to read. I was aware that my voice was high-pitched and a little louder than usual. I looked at them quickly to see if they were listening.

Raymond was looking down at his copy. His fingers were tapping on his chair and the sound became very loud and disturbing.

Beverly sat frozen on the couch next to the door.

The letter began with "Dear Beverly."

I'd written the first paragraph to let Beverly know that her work with the university was appreciated. "First and foremost, I value your contributions to the program and I believe you are very committed to your work."[6]

Raymond's tapping became louder. Beverly's hands were clasped and the letter was sitting on top of her pink notepad. She was looking at it, but I wasn't sure she was reading it.

I continued reading. "Please know, Beverly, that I want to support and help you as much as I possible can. Please know that I am concerned about you."

I began to experience a change. My initial sinking feeling began to dissipate and my heart started beating steadily with a rush of adrenaline. I finally felt in charge.

Glancing up to look at each of them squarely in the eye, I turned the page to read the essential paragraph of the letter.

> As director, I feel I must provide a written record of a concern that I'm bringing to your attention. Here are the facts: (1) On November 18, 2005, an item was purchased that appears fraudulent. The item, a DVD mini-camcorder is valued to be $1,400.74. (2) Beverly, you purchased this item without getting proper approval. The item is an inappropriate purchase for our program and appears to be for personal use. (3) The certification signature is yours. This clearly is not a legitimate business expense.

I looked up at Beverly then took another breath, shifted my weight because my foot was falling asleep again, and paused just before reading the final sentence. "Using program funds and resources for personal gain is a violation of university policy," I read with my voice rising. "This is clearly a misuse of funds," and then continued, "Embezzlement cannot be tolerated by the University," I read, looking directly at Beverly and punctuating my statement with great anguish.

I then handed Beverly and Raymond a copy of the purchase order, the essential parts highlighted in yellow. Beverly's name and signature, her certification, and her handwritten words "pick up from vendor," were all identified.

I paused only to put the letter back on my lap so I could observe the two other people in the room still gazing down at the words in the letter. I quickly turned to Beverly, caught her eye, and asked, "Beverly, where's the DVD camcorder?"

"It's in my garage" Beverly replied.

I held my breath fearing that she'd bolt or burst into tears. I was quite relieved and startled that she confessed so quickly and without a struggle!

Beverly stared blankly, not showing any emotion, and not looking at either of us.

Raymond kept staring at the letter, stunned and silent. He wasn't moving at all and certainly not looking at me. One hand was on his chair, his fingers still drumming. He'd dropped his pen while I was reading the letter. I noted it was too far to pick up and that he didn't even try to recover it.

As he was reading the letter, he turned in his chair slightly away from me. His face was white, and he was uncharacteristically quiet. He lowered his head and was shaking it in what appeared to be disbelief. I was relieved that he finally got the message about Beverly. I thought to myself: He must be very shocked!

"It's in your garage." I repeated what she'd said.

"Yes, the DVD camcorder is in my garage," Beverly acknowledged.

Raymond finally emerged from his stupor. "Is it still in the box?" he asked, still looking down at the letter.

She nodded.

I was pretty sure that the DVD camcorder wasn't in a box and probably wasn't even in her garage, but at least she admitted that it was in her possession. I'd recalled back in December that Beverly told me that she filmed her son's basketball games. I was pretty confident that she'd purchased this item for herself and was using it regularly. *It's called stealing*, I reminded myself.

Raymond was now looking directly at Beverly sympathetically and as if he was trying to catch her eye. Her posture changed. She was now bent forward with her head in her hands, a sight I'd never expected to see.

I had put Kleenex in my briefcase in case she began to cry, but there weren't any tears.

"Beverly, do you want to tell us your side of the story?" I asked cautiously.

He looks desolate. They must be having some sort "thing," I thought to myself.

Beverly looked like she was getting up the courage to speak, but just as she was about to open her mouth, Raymond interrupted her.

"Let me see if I can offer what I think Beverly might say. People who are hard workers often feel overlooked and underpaid. It is human nature to feel one deserves more. And with the holidays, and this kind of personal stress, people can behave out of character. We all know Beverly to be honest. Beverly will return or pay back the university the cost of the camcorder."

Beverly, still silent, paused briefly, and then folded up the letter.

"Has this ever happened before?" I asked, hoping to regain control of the meeting.

"This is the first and only time, and it will never happen again," she answered simply without showing any emotion and staring straight ahead. "I promise that this will never happen again. I take full responsibility," Beverly added, then stood up to go.

"We need to revise your job description," I told Beverly as she turned toward the door. I wondered how she was able to purchase equipment without my signature. *This wasn't going to happen again.*

As she turned to open the door, I asked one final question.

"Beverly, is this the camcorder you used to film your son's basketball games?" Her son was an assistant coach for a Sacramento high school team.

She nodded and mumbled a yes as she opened the door. She then walked out as poised and dignified as ever. I even saw her straighten and raise her head as she quietly shut the door behind her.

Raymond and I stayed in his office. I waited for him to say something but he remained silent.

"I was shocked when I discovered this," I said, hoping to get a response from him.

"Are you sure she did this?" he replied abruptly, almost accusingly. "You know that falsely accusing someone is a serious offense."

Hadn't he noticed that she'd already confessed!? In fact, he didn't even ask me how I found out.

"Don't worry," I responded, "I did my homework."

I could tell he wasn't in the mood to talk, so I stood up to go. As I left his office, he handed me back the letter and the purchase order.

When I returned to my office, I avoided Beverly. She stayed until five o'clock, then left in a hurry. I revised the March 2 letter to include our confidential discussion, specifically that Beverly had agreed to repay the university and specified which of her job duties would be changed. I sent it to Beverly and copied Raymond. Although the first letter was private and personal, this revised letter became my official response showing that I'd reported the misuse of funds to the department chair, discussed it with the employee, and had determined and taken corrective action.

Later, when I went over the meeting, a lot of unanswered questions kept popping into my head: *Why hadn't he asked how I found out about the DVD camcorder? Why did he give me back the letter? Why didn't he congratulate me on how I handled the situation? And what holiday stress? She stole it in November!*

I reviewed my tête-à-tête with Raymond after Beverly left his office. It was very brief and all I could recall was his "Are you sure?" question. I kept thinking about it the rest of the day.

Why did he react like that?

It was now Friday, and Beverly was not in the office. She'd requested a vacation day long before our meeting, and I was quite relieved that I didn't have to interact with her. I was still angry that she'd done this to me, to the program, and to the university. However, Raymond felt differently about it.

"Are you sure?" he asked me again when we met to discuss the letter I'd written documenting our meeting on March 2.

"Absolutely," I replied gritting my teeth. "She told us it was in her garage, remember?"

"Look," he added, "I told you before, Beverly is stressed. This is no big deal. You're overreacting. This kind of thing happens all the time at UC. It's an error in judgment. I've been through this with many employees. This isn't anything world-shattering, my friend."

"Not on my watch," I said to him defiantly. I asked him if I could suspend Beverly on a temporary basis.

"No!" he said flat-footedly. "As chair and your supervisor, this is my responsibility." He was now standing up.

"You owe it to your friendship with Beverly and to the program to try to find a way to forgive her," he interjected. "You're too hard on people, and this is why you have so many problems." He paused letting that sink in. "We both owe it to Beverly to give her a second chance."

I said nothing. I was stuck on the idea that this happened "all the time" at the university. I wanted to ask him who the other employees were. I did hear him say I was too hard on people, and maybe he was right, but that wasn't the point. *She stole, for god's sake*, I thought. Before I could say anything, he continued.

"She said she'd pay back the money to the university. You've written an official letter for the files. Let's wait and see. We're giving her a second chance, that's my decision. I'm convinced that she'll buckle down to work now."

"Now, at least she must be required to follow the appropriate procedures and get my approval before any future purchases."

Raymond agreed.

I wasn't too happy about giving Beverly a second chance, but I was persuaded that her "poor judgment" as Raymond called it, "was deserving of some compassionate understanding." I also figured that we'd put a stop to the possibility of this incident repeating itself.

On Monday, Beverly arrived very early to work. She made quite a show of working very hard, even bending over backwards to be agreeable, cautiously courteous, and pleasant to me. She reminded me of my upcoming nutrition meetings, prepared reports before I asked for them, and even tried to soothe me with intermittent flattery. She also initiated a conference call to discuss next year's budget with several university accountants. This was a big and welcome surprise. I always had to nag her to get guidance from university budget experts. My discomfort about the incident with the camcorder gradually began to subside. Maybe I had overreacted to this one-time transgression.

The next day Beverly told me she was going to Fry's after work to return the item. I had my doubts, but was curious to see if she could persuade Fry's to take back a used DVD camcorder. She promised to let me know the following day. I was scheduled to work from home the next two days.

She didn't answer her telephone all day Wednesday.

Thursday morning I received an email from her indicating something I'd already known. Fry's had a fourteen-day return policy. In the email sent to both Raymond and me, she included a cock-and-bull story that the camcorder wasn't purchased for her but ordered for Marge Bell, our Madera program manager. Beverly said that she forgot that she'd done that. Trying to weasel out of paying back the funds, she forwarded us two emails: first, one from Marge who'd requested a digital camera in August 2005; and second, her response to Marge, denying the purchase on September 5, even stating that the purchase of a digital camera was inappropriate. Besides being the wrong item, digital camera not DVD camcorder, and her admission that this purchase was inappropriate, the purchase dates didn't jive. She wasn't making any sense. Obviously, even if what she said had any validity, how could she explain her admission that the camcorder was in her garage?

Convinced that Beverly was trying to create a scenario to cover up her misuse of funds, I immediately phoned her, and we had a rather heated discussion on the phone. She was irrational and refused to listen. Then she told me another crazy story. According to Beverly, Raymond agreed to buy the camcorder for the department and said that the cost would be transferred to his account. I hung up and sent both of them an email to the effect that Beverly had already agreed on March 2 to repay the money to the university, and she needed to honor that commitment. I got into my car and sped up to Davis, determined to get a personal check from Beverly. I asked her to write a letter admitting to the inappropriate purchase. I was surprised that she did both without a fuss. She wrote:

> March 9, 2006
>
> Dear Amy,
> I cannot begin to explain what happened to me about the purchase of the DVD camcorder. I must have had a hard time over the holidays. I regret this mistake. Please know that it will never happen again.
> Thanks for your understanding.
>
> Beverly E. Benford
> cc: Raymond Savage

I noticed that she used the exact wording that Raymond had suggested during our March 2 meeting.

Beverly reluctantly gave me a check made out to the Regents of the University of California and said she didn't have the money in her account but she would next month. Could I hold the check?

I agreed. Matters would be much worse if her check bounced.

In any case, in the short term, things didn't get worse. They actually improved. I revised Beverly's job description, making clear that I had to approve all invoices she put through for payment, and continued to monitor her, waiting for any sign of danger. Surprisingly contrite, she actually came into my office crying, telling me tearfully how sorry she was that she'd let me down. I reminded her that the issue was really about letting the program down.

However, at the end of March, when I told her I was taking the check to the university's cashier office, she said "Oh, please

Amy. I still don't have the money."

She told me that she'd requested a loan from her credit union, and she showed me the paperwork to prove it.

Then, on March 28, Beverly told me her loan was denied and I'd have to wait until mid-April for her to get the cash. Then she left the office headed home. I had the feeling she wasn't taking this seriously and was trying to get me to back down.

I went to her office and found a stack of dusty purchase orders, most from 2005 when I was on sabbatical, on her desk—none of them with my signature. I went through each one very carefully. I was relieved to find that all of them were for appropriate purchases of office supplies and small equipment for the program. My faith in Beverly was beginning to be restored. *Maybe I did overreact*, I thought as I was about to go home.

But before I left, I saw another dusty stack of emails in her printer and decided to look through those. Finding another questionable purchase order, I noted that this one had the same red flag, a vaguely described item from Fry's Electronics with the words "pick up from vendor" clearly typed on the form.

The item, Onkyo MC-35 Tech, costing $399.99, stuck out like a sore thumb amid a bunch of legitimate items on the purchase order.

Finding a Web site for Fry's Electronics was easy. Finding out that the Onkyo MC-35 Tech was a stereo system was alarming. This was obviously not a legitimate program expense.

I arranged to meet with Raymond about a week later, on April 6. I told him there had been another misuse of funds and showed him the purchase order. He pointed out that the stereo purchase occurred on March 3, 2005.

"This is a long time ago, well before the camcorder," he said furiously, shoving it back into my hands. I wasn't sure how to understand this.

"We agreed that if this should happen again, we'd officially report it," I reminded him.

"But it didn't happen *again*," he said, angrily emphasizing the word again.

"Raymond," I said pointedly, "what she said doesn't jibe with the facts. Beverly said that her purchasing the DVD camcorder without my approval was a one-time event. It doesn't matter which purchase was first or second. It's all stealing!"

"I'm going to repeat myself," said Raymond standing up. "This purchase doesn't count." He stared at me in contempt and then let me have it.

"It looks to me like you're trying to sabotage Beverly and the whole program."

"And why would I do that?" I fired back at him.

We continued to argue but made no headway. I asked his permission to go to the next step of reporting this to the dean's office and the USDA. He reminded me that this was his responsibility, not mine.

Again he accused me of "having it in for Beverly."

I told him that I'd gone ahead and documented this second incident in a letter.

"I'm going to send it to her tomorrow. Here's your copy," I said and handed him my letter dated April 7.

"This letter serves as an official warning that University policy has been compromised by activities #1-4 . . . and serves as a written notice of intent to take temporary corrective action. . ." the letter began. After the description of the misuse of funds, the letter continued with " . . . your title will be changed . . . you will be under direct supervision . . . will not be allowed . . . any financial . . . purchasing . . . hiring . . . personnel decisions . . . warning period of four months to determine if permanent or continuing corrective action is warranted . . ."

Raymond growled. He was about to say something then changed his mind and handed me back my letter.

"Okay," was all he said as I turned and left him standing there empty-handed.

Later that day, he replied to the email I'd sent earlier with the letter attached. "This is right on target," he wrote.

A few days later, Beverly brought in the stereo. I locked it up in the office and kept the key myself. She was stripped of all her duties as the program administrator.

Maybe I'd finally convinced him to take this seriously.

Beverly also replied to my letter. She finally had gotten the message!

> Hi Amy and Raymond,
>
> The attached letter causes me to be highly emotional . . . I prefer not to talk about it until I have some time to compose myself and think about how this will impact me and my future . . .
>
> I want you both to know that I have taken full responsibility for my actions. I am ashamed and most of all embarrassed. This will NEVER happen again! Ever since our first meeting, I have taken measures not to . . .
>
> Thanks for your understanding of my feelings.
>
> Beverly

Meanwhile, I was still waiting to cash her check. In the middle of April she told me that she had used all her cash to pay her taxes and now didn't have the money. I went to Raymond and he once again accused me of making too big a deal about this.

"She'll pay it back. Be compassionate, and relax. You need to give her a little while longer," he cautioned.

Then he added, "How about having the department pay for this? Then she'd have more time to pay back the department or whatever is necessary."

I said no.

Then, seemingly out of the blue, the tone of Beverly's behavior began to change. She wrote me a very assertive, almost confrontational, email—and copied Raymond on it—asking me to return her personal check and telling me she would get me a cashier's check.

I politely refused, which created more tension. During the following days, she began to behave erratically, one day charming and friendly, the next angry and cold. Toward the end of April, she actually misled me, giving me the wrong time and date for a meeting in Sacramento. I ended up spending several hours pacing back and forth in front of a locked building. While doing so, however, I concluded that Beverly had no intention of repaying the university. On April 27 and then again on May 2 I sent emails to Raymond to tell him that I felt that I was compromising my integrity by not reporting the incident to a higher authority, the dean's office or human resources.

On May 2, Raymond telephoned me. He was seething. Before I could even bring up the issue of doing the right thing, he angrily told me that Beverly'd been complaining to a number of faculty in the department about me.

"Who?"

"For one, Dr. Stone, Fred. Then there's your friend, Dr. Small, not to mention Dr. Heller and Dr. Frost. I could go on, but I think you can see that a significant number of individuals are now concerned. To be honest Amy, the issue isn't just with Beverly. Some of the folks you've been working with find you too difficult. I've tried to convince folks that the program is having a crisis and it's been an exceptionally difficult time for you. You really need to relax!"

"Difficult time for me? Crisis? What on earth do you mean?"

"Look, my friend," he began, "this isn't a conspiracy. You need to take a deep breath. Believe me, you don't want to get people up in arms and start a war. Accusations have been flying in multiple directions. Trust me that some of them are directed at you. Beverly's very popular—folks here really like her. Lighten up. She's going to get the money for you."

"For me? Raymond, it's the university's money! What kind of accusations? What do you mean?" Oblivious to my concerns, he cleared his throat and raised his voice.

"Beverly's been crying to Fred and to others that you want her to go to jail!" he announced dramatically. Unfazed, I continued my line of inquiry.

"Did she tell them about the camcorder?" It seemed odd that Beverly would talk to people about the theft. *Shouldn't she be ashamed? Why would she tell people? Jail? What's going on?*

"I'm not sure what's been actually said to whom. I just know that this is getting blown all out of proportion. Consult with Fred and do so quickly."

I stiffly agreed and said good-bye.

On May 8, at two in the afternoon, I met with Dr. Fred Stone, a rather burly guy with salt-and-pepper gray hair, large quizzical dark eyes, a great sense of humor, and a huge resume. He'd been in the department over thirty years and was well-versed in university politics. He assumed the role of vice-chair when Raymond was out of town.

"Raymond suggested I talk to you about Beverly," I said. "Do you know what's going on?" I was a little wary because Fred was a loyal supporter of Raymond's.

"Beverly's been here belly-aching. Personally, I don't like her. I have concerns about Beverly. She's not been forthcoming."

"About what?" I asked suddenly intrigued.

"She's been here twice now, sitting in that very chair," he said pointing to the chair I was sitting in, "telling me that you're creating a hostile work environment."

"You've got to be kidding!"

"The first visit, she cried and cried. According to Beverly," he said seriously, "you accused her of stealing equipment!" He stopped and watched for my reaction.

"Go on," I said calmly, looking him directly in the eye.

"When I asked if there was any truth to your accusation, she said absolutely not! She was beside herself in anger that I'd questioned her. A day or so later, she came up here again, showed me some confusing emails, and again tried to convince me of her innocence. She said that she'd purchased something for the program, and you're making a big stink about it. She said you called it stealing. She was crying the whole time."

"Did she tell you what 'it' was?" I asked.

"A camera for some program in Madera County, I think." He looked a little puzzled, then continued. "She said that you're trying to make it look like she stole it for herself."

I pulled out the purchase order that I brought with me to the meeting.

"Actually Fred, 'it' was a Canon Optura DVD mini-camcorder that cost $1,400.74! A camcorder isn't a camera. And it wasn't for the program. Raymond can vouch for that. He was there when she confessed to buying it for herself to film her son playing basketball." He looked at the purchase order and raised his eyebrows.

"Are you noting her signature all over the page? She approved it, certified it, and picked it up." I said, pointing to her three signatures.

"Whoa," he said startled. "Anything else?" he asked still staring at the purchase order.

"Yes, here's her repayment check and her letter acknowledging this purchase was improper." I said handing him each of the documents and watching for his response. Clearly this was the first time he'd heard of these documents.

"And here's a second purchase from March 2005. I'm surprised Raymond didn't talk to you about this?"

He didn't speak but his face was very eloquent. "Beverly's made some provocative statements," he said. His outrage was finally showing.

"Provocative?" I asked, curious as to what she might have told him.

"She's arrogant and obfuscating. When I asked her why you would accuse her of stealing and if you had any evidence of that, she became downright furious, gave me a dirty look, and plowed out of here, slamming my door. This isn't the behavior of a happy camper."

When he left to make copies, I remembered something that

Beverly said about Fred long ago when she'd met with him about the plastic plant. *Fred, oh he's so full of himself. He doesn't know what he's talking about, although he does love to talk. I won't be wasting my time with him, vice-chair or not!*

I didn't share this tidbit. Fred returned with his copies and sat down to use his computer. Searching the accounting database on his computer, he looked for more purchases from Fry's Electronics, but didn't find anything else.

"Two purchases in 2005 is bad enough. She has to go. I don't care what Raymond says," was his final statement. He assured me that he'd take care of the reporting process to get the "termination ball rolling."

"What about Raymond?" I asked tentatively, noting that he'd not answered my question about Raymond's knowledge of Beverly's wrongdoing.

"Raymond is naïve," he confided in me. "Beverly's been a good friend to the department, and he appreciates her," he added, indicating that she'd helped a variety of folks and was very popular.

"Popular?" I asked, wondering about Raymond's relationship with her.

"Oh, the usual things," he said to me, winking. Then turning serious, he added. "But she's gone too far. This has to end. Raymond's too involved to see clearly." He indicated that he'd be meeting with the dean shortly but said that they were "very slow and to be patient."

Before I left his office, he suggested I talk to Darci Small, another colleague in the department. He didn't say why; he just said that Beverly'd been crying in her office as well.

"I'm going to see her right now," I said as I left his office. I felt greatly relieved. *Finally, someone with clout's going to do something!* I said to myself on my way to Darci's office.

As I approached her open door, I thought about my relationship with Darci. Dr. Darci Small, a petite and competent young woman, was very friendly and had a great sense of humor. We'd have lunch together and frequently kid around, often making fun of ourselves. She'd share stories of her toddler son and the frustrations of her assistant-level faculty position. She was someone I enjoyed talking to, and I admired her mentoring style with her students. With a wonderful laugh and warm eyes, everyone loved Darci and I enjoyed her friendship. We both shared a desire to help poor families. I was surprised that Beverly was confiding in her. Beverly knew that I considered Darci a good friend and highly regarded her.

I put my head into her office and found Darci sitting at her desk.

"Hi Darci, do you have a minute?"

She smiled and looked at her watch. "Just a sec, I need to send this email. Have a seat."

I shut her door, mumbling something about the noise in the hall, and sat down, looking at the photo of her three-year-old, mostly toothless, son on her desk. I waited until Darci hit the send button and turned to face me.

"Darci, I just spoke to Fred and he suggested that I meet with you."

She looked shocked and anxious.

"Fred told me that Beverly's been in your office crying," I said then paused to wait for her to speak. Although a little abrupt, I was in a hurry to find out what was going on.

"Yes, Beverly's been crying to me, actually sobbing," she said looking serious. "She made me promise not to tell you," she added looking awkward. "She told me and Roberta Heller that you were mistreating her. Roberta is really pissed." Dr. Roberta Heller was another faculty member.

"What does she mean by mistreatment?" I was startled.

"Beverly said you accused her of stealing!" Darci exclaimed with great anguish.

I couldn't tell her what was going on but I did want to say something. "You don't really believe that I'd falsely accuse someone, do you?" I looked at her, firmly convinced that my relationship with her would mean something. Then I continued. "As your friend and colleague, please listen to me carefully, this is very serious and complicated. Fred's going to handle it, so please try to stay out of it."

"Okay," she mumbled, turning pale and looking frightened. There was no rhyme or reason for Darci to get involved in this mess!

I was determined to get Beverly to pay back the money to the university to show that she was seriously taking responsibility for what she did. People make mistakes, as Raymond continually preached to me, but part of moving past those mistakes is accepting responsibility and repairing any damage done.

I also wondered about Beverly's relationship with Raymond. This "thing" that she had with him was puzzling. Raymond's behavior toward her was more than just professional concern or empathy.

Most of May passed with Beverly being civil yet trying hard to avoid me. We managed to finish the work on the next year's contract. Though she mostly acted as though all was well with the world, one day she broke down and sobbed in my office. I took this as a good sign, and attributed it to remorse, even thinking she could now get help. However, I was completely wrong.

On June 5th, Beverly made a mistake. Wholly unaware, she accidentally sent me an email that was meant for Raymond's eyes only. It seems her alligator tears were simply part an elaborate cover-up.

"I found half the money. I just want to get her off my back," said her email to Raymond. Raymond was out of town. I immediately wrote Raymond an email that he could receive while away from the office.

"This is totally unacceptable," I wrote, and again expressed my desire to seek counsel from the dean's office or internal auditing. He responded quickly by Blackberry that I should follow the chain of command and consult again with the vice-chair of the department, Dr. Stone.

On June 5 I met again with Fred and told him that Beverly still hadn't paid the university back for the equipment she had bought for herself. I asked him directly what had happened at the dean's office.

"I think what you're doing is reasonable," he told me, without addressing my question about the dean's office. He also indicated he'd been very busy.

"The next step is to give Beverly an ultimatum about the check. I'd write her a letter notifying her that embezzlement is clearly grounds for termination," Fred stated.

On June 5, he sent me an email and copied Raymond. ". . . this does not bode well . . . embezzlement is clearly grounds for termination and unless something is done . . . it will be turned over to . . . USDA legal staff for further action." This was music to my ears!

Fred then sent Raymond an email, and copied me. "Let's end this!! . . . Beverly has boxed herself into a corner . . ."

Fred then coached me through a series of steps required by university protocol to terminate an employee. The first was a letter of expectation. I'd already done that.

Step two was a warning letter telling the employee that they hadn't met the expectations. I'd done that one, too.

Step three was a second warning. I drafted the letter, which Fred read, liked, and approved. He asked me to sign it with a copy to him. I gave Beverly the letter on Monday, June 12.

> Dear Beverly,
>
> This letter is to communicate in writing a second warning. As of June 12, 2006, you have not complied with the required action in the first warning letter of April 7 . . . Embezzlement is the act of fraudulently appropriating for personal use or gain money or goods entrusted to one's care and management. The documentation of the items purchased, your

> admission to the purchase, as well as your ⠀
> agreement to reimburse the program by June 1
> has already been reported . . . This letter is your
> final warning. If compliance . . . not . . . com-
> pleted . . . your employment will be terminated
> . . .

Not surprisingly, that very day, Beverly sent me an email that I could now cash her check; she had finally found the money to pay back the university.

Greatly relieved, and feeling supported by Fred, I began to relax, believing that my uphill battle with Raymond was finally over. Fred would now have to turn the issue over to the dean's office for them to finalize. Beverly, however, didn't even blink an eye. Oddly enough, she left town on a hastily planned vacation.

It was now July, and Beverly was still out of town. Luckily she and I had managed to complete the contract for 2006 before everything had become really messy. The next year's contract was now safely in the hands of Carolyn Diamond, our CDSS contact.

I was scheduled to have abdominal surgery for skin cancer at the beginning of July but postponed it until July 31. I was concerned about being out of the office, not knowing what Beverly might do in my absence.

The surgery was successful. While I was recovering and working at home, I didn't hear any word from Fred about the dean's office. Beverly had returned to work and was keeping a very low profile. At least that's what I thought.

Toward the end of my recovery, three members of my administrative staff—Dolores, Frances, and Marcia—called me at home to tell me that Beverly was signing purchase orders again.

One faculty colleague, Dr. Cindy Slovis, a large woman with a no-nonsense style and politically-correct attitudes, told me that Beverly was behaving badly, getting angry and admonishing her staff publicly. She provided clear examples of Beverly being intimidating and threatening to both Dolores and Frances. I spoke to Cindy by telephone.

"Beverly yelled at Dolores about a purchase order for a computer," Cindy told me when I called her on the phone. "She said that you were not going to approve the computer purchase. She's like a ticking time bomb. You've got to do something."

"Any suggestions?" I said, unsure if Cindy knew of Beverly's past transgressions. One thing I did know: Beverly hadn't sent me any purchase orders to approve.

"I spoke to Fred, who's now risen from the vice-chair to departmental chair. It was announced this month," she said, indicating I probably didn't know. "He's so passive," exclaimed Cindy who had a flair for drama.

Cindy also indicated that Fred with his "dinosaur mentality" was often slow to act. She convinced me to have a face-to-face meeting with him. However, she didn't mention anything about embezzlement. And she was correct—I hadn't received any announcement that Fred was now the official chair.

"You've got to get Fred on your side," she cautioned. "Otherwise, you'll get nowhere and most likely end up in hot water. Fred's not one for action," said Cindy. "Fred's a nice guy, but he hates controversy," she added. *No kidding*, I said to myself.

I told Cindy to leave the computer purchase request in my box at Davis. I wondered what other paperwork managed to elude my approval because of Beverly. My plan was to return to work and relieve Beverly of her last remaining job function— supervising. I documented the previous incidents in a letter addressed to Beverly. I sent the letter to Fred for his review and arranged to meet with him. I figured if the department wasn't going to do anything, I'd personally make sure that she'd pose no more danger to the program.

I met with Fred the morning of Thursday, August 24, 2006, my first day back. Surprisingly friendly and pleasant, he approved my plan of removing Beverly's supervisory role. I asked about the dean's office. He mumbled something about this being a departmental issue that had already been resolved.

"She's paid back the university. I don't want this to reflect on the department or the people here. It's been adequately dealt with," he said quite firmly and then stopped abruptly.

Annoyed that he'd backed down, I said I was planning on giving Beverly the letter at two, and I expected she'd become angry and might create a scene.

"Oh, yes, she'll be angry," he said nodding in agreement. "She's already spreading some really good gossip." He was smiling broadly, and his eyes danced at my dazed expression.

"Good gossip?" I didn't really want to know, but I could see he was dying to tell me. "Okay Fred, what's the scoop?" I asked.

"She's telling people that you have stomach cancer with a poor prognosis," he said watching closely for my reaction.

"Wishful thinking," I said, laughing. Amused, I got up to leave, feeling triumphant. I noticed he was chuckling as I turned and waved good-bye. Yes, Fred probably didn't want to make waves at the dean's office, but at least he was still on my side.

Two of Beverly's staff—Ginny Buckner, her administrative assistant, and Ryan Holt, the programmer—were in the office that Thursday, August 24. I first met with Ginny, a lovely, dedicated woman with a friendly, warm smile, but also, according to Beverly, her best friend and "sidekick." I wanted to warn Ginny that Beverly would get a letter that very afternoon and might become angry.

"Ginny," I said as she sat in my office, "what I have to say to you is highly confidential. I'm relieving Beverly of her supervisory responsibilities today. I'm going to be your supervisor for the next two weeks. You're now going to report directly to me."

"Does Beverly know this?" Ginny asked, her eyes getting big.

"Not yet. I wanted to let you know first and ask you to go home now. She might be upset, and I don't want anyone to get the brunt of a possible negative response."

"You bet she'll be upset. No question about that!" Ginny then became alarmed. "Beverly drove me to work today," she added looking nervous.

"Don't worry. I'll ask Ryan to give you a ride home. I'm going to speak to him now and ask him to go home before two, when I'm going to give Beverly the letter." Ginny looked surprisingly happy at the idea. "Now, mum's the word," I said. Ginny grinned sheepishly.

Ryan, our big-hearted and talented "tech guy," came into my office. I told him I'd be meeting with Beverly at two and that he and Ginny should quietly leave just before then. He said he'd be happy to give Ginny a lift. He smiled and thanked me then quietly put his head down. For a brief second, I thought he was going to burst into tears.

At two o'clock, Beverly knocked on my door and walked in. I asked her to sit down and then handed her the letter. She read it quickly and didn't seem too surprised. I wanted to be sure to give both Ginny and Ryan enough time to leave, so I continued meeting with Beverly for another ten minutes. She was very antsy and kept asking, "Can I go now? I've got work to do."

I told her that I'd given staff the afternoon off and that Ryan was taking Ginny home. At this point, I saw a flash of anger, but she remained quiet. She then requested to also go home and I agreed.

I went home that night, pleased that things were finally getting resolved. At eight that evening, the telephone rang.

"Hello."

"Hi, it's Ginny, I finally found your home number." She was sounding anxious.

"I need to tell you something," she said.

Ginny said that she was so happy that I was her new boss. "Ryan and I cheered all the way home!" she told me.

"You're my boss now, right?" she asked sounding tentative.

"Yes," I answered intrigued.

"Well, new boss, are you sitting down?"

"Yep." I heard her gulp. A few seconds later, she took the

plunge.

"Beverly's been getting travel reimbursements for trips she never took," Ginny said. "I've done her travel, so has Tessa, and we both knew she wasn't traveling to those places. She'd fire me if she knew I told you. Don't tell her I told you, but that's why Tessa resigned." Ginny became very quiet.

After we both caught our breath, I asked Ginny where I could find the travel documentation.

"You won't find her travel documents in our office. She takes the office copy home. You'll have to go to accounts payable to see them," Ginny told me bravely.

Beverly rarely traveled, at the most one trip a year to the national meeting. I'd never seen any travel vouchers for her. She was a budget analyst, and she didn't need to go anywhere. She never attended our nutrition meetings.

"Accounts payable?" I was trying to figure out if I'd ever been there.

"The office is on the other side of the freeway. By the way, you need to talk to the manager, because her travel vouchers will be hard to find. Beverly always had me do her travel reimbursement on an emergency basis so she'd get the money faster. Dr. Savage approved all of them. It's a lot of money for just sitting on her butt in Davis." Ginny sounded appropriately irate.

"How much?" I asked Ginny wondering what she'd say.

"Hmmm. Well at a rate of about five hundred dollars a month for the last year, maybe more in the previous year . . . what would that be?"

"Wow!" I was startled.

"Yep, that's a bunch of money," Ginny said, as we both gulped. She wished me luck as we said our good-byes.

I tossed and turned all night, barely able to sleep. I was worried that somehow the evidence was going to be lost or destroyed. Early Friday morning, on August 25, 2006, I drove up to Davis at sunrise and waited in the parking lot until eight. When accounts payable opened, I asked to meet with the accounting office manager, Anna Strong. I stayed in the waiting room until Anna was available to meet with me.

I told Anna that I was doing a random travel audit on one of my employees. She looked up the information on her computer, and it agreed with what Ginny reported. All Beverly's travel reimbursements were "emergency reimbursement," and these were filed in a separate storage area in the building. Anna told me it would take a while to locate them, and I agreed to wait. I didn't want to take up a lot of her time, so we selected a couple of vouchers to copy and review. For someone not traveling, her reimbursement for each of these months was enormous—over five hundred dollars each.

It was easy to discover that my employee was falsifying travel to the tune of a thousand dollars a month! I reviewed only two months of claims and found that most of her expenses were mileage reimbursement for fictitious trips. Ginny had indicated that this had been going on for at least twelve and maybe as many as twenty-four months, so this was obviously just the tip of the iceberg. My new estimate of the travel fraud was twenty thousand dollars!

I had no trouble ascertaining that these two months of travel were falsified. Most of the trips corresponded to ones I actually took, identical in locations, dates, and expenses. Trouble was, Beverly never accompanied me to these nutrition meetings. There was also one completely fabricated 560-mile trip from Davis to southern California to pick up a "broken computer."

I immediately called Fred and told him I urgently needed to see him. It was now almost two o'clock on Friday afternoon. We met for forty-five minutes.

"Oh, yes, we've all been wondering about her travel," Fred said candidly, looking over my copies of the falsified vouchers. "One of the department's staff actually refused to type them and brought the issue to our attention."

"Now we can fire her," I said.

"Hold your horses, this will take a while," he answered. He mentioned that Beverly had already called him about my letter.

"She's pretty upset with you," he warned. "Raymond and I are meeting with her next week. This travel stuff will have to wait."

"Wait? We can't wait." He looked angry. I stopped pushing. How could I diplomatically tell my boss that he must be blind, dense, or completely out of his mind? *Doesn't he see what's going on here? What's wrong with him?*

Deflated, I watched him leave his office to make copies down the hall of the fraudulent vouchers. After he left, I wondered about Beverly's travel being previously questioned. Why wasn't I told and consulted? Who questioned it? Did this happen when I was off having surgery?

I'd managed to calm down by the time he returned and casually asked him if Raymond was aware of her questionable travel vouchers. "Oh, yes," he said looking serious, "very aware."

He handed me back the evidence. "Don't worry. I'll consult with the dean's office next week," he said and plopped down in his chair.

"Today," I said. "You have to do this today," I repeated, trying again to convince him that this was urgent.

Catching my drift, he cautioned me about acting alone, even suggested I was misguided and could get into big trouble.

"This is my decision, not yours," he began. "It will take time. The university moves slowly. It's now almost four o'clock on a Friday afternoon. No one's around. You don't know the ins and outs of the university," he said, staring at me with his nostrils flaring.

"Come on, it's only a couple of thousand dollars," he continued trying to sound persuasive. "Raymond's right, you do need to lighten up. You're making much ado about nothing," he interjected defensively. "Sit tight, do nothing, and wait until you hear from me."

Before I left, he continued, in case I hadn't understood. "Let me remind you again that this is my decision. I'll call you over the weekend," he concluded without much emotion. Exhausted, I handed him my home phone number, slowly rose from my chair, and walked out without saying another word.

On the staircase on my way back to my office, I felt haunted.

There was something odd about his demeanor, I thought, something's missing. *Where's his outrage? Like Raymond, he's not going to do anything. Oh yes, I almost forgot, he is doing something. He's meeting with Beverly!*

Feeling more and more disgusted, I got into my car and sped home. *Beverly must be stopped*, I promised myself as I got out of my car at home.

I felt like I'd reached my boiling point. She'd been caught stealing equipment, and now money! Maybe he was protecting Raymond from some scandal, but scandal or not, this is wrong! My pile of evidence of embezzlement and fraud should have made him angry, outraged. Instead, he tells me the university moves slowly. Frankly, I didn't believe him. My faith in both of these two powerful men was officially gone. Departmental chair—humph!

Enough! I told myself. *I've had enough.*

5 | Moral Outrage

After my return home, I found some relief from my obsessing over Fred's demand that I do nothing by writing out the whole saga. Beginning with my meeting with Raymond on March 2 and continuing through my agonizing finish with Fred, I wrote and wrote. Cutting and pasting letters, emails, and notes from meetings and telephone calls, I filled pages and pages with all the sordid details.

"There's nothing wrong with me," I said after reading what I'd written, my mood elevated by a fair amount of alcohol. I had written forty pages.

It made no sense that Fred would protect Beverly, whom he'd labeled dishonest, and I believed his dislike of her was genuine. What wasn't clear was why Fred had become so wishy-washy. Was he protecting superstar Raymond, his friend, out of some misguided loyalty? Was there some inappropriate alliance between Ray and Bev?

I'd already spent too much time hoping I was wrong about Beverly. I wanted to see her as Raymond had suggested, troubled and stressed-out by money problems. But people with money problems don't necessarily steal! I've worked with low-income families now for twenty-six years, and I'd never witnessed this kind of behavior. The money she stole was intended to help poor families!

The travel fraud tipped the balance. And now, putting Fred and Raymond in the mix, I had to wonder what kind of people would cover up the truth so callously?

I summarized my forty-page document into a factual two-page report without everybody's speculations, veiled threats, strange behavior, gossip, and perplexing questions. I signed it and went to bed. Feeling tense and exhausted, I finally fell into a deep sleep and had the most unbelievable dream!

I'm supposed to take a test at Davis. I feel anxious and leave early in the morning. I'm driving in the dark. My car starts to sputter and slows down. Clutching the steering wheel tightly, my foot pressing the gas pedal to the floor, I try to go faster. I watch the speedometer drop from sixty to forty, then down to twenty. I'm barely moving. The highway is eerie, cold, dark, and empty. I finally see the Davis exit but now I can't turn the steering wheel! It won't budge. My arms are hurting and getting heavy. I see a child on the side of the road yelling and waving at me. I try to stop, but now the brake pedal isn't working . . .

I woke up, even more certain now that no-action Fred was stalling. If things were going to get put right, I'd have to do something.

I found envelopes and addressed them to everyone higher than the department chairs. Reading over my report one more time before making seven copies, I sealed the deal!

August 25, 2006

Misuse of University Funds and Embezzlement by UC employee Beverly Benford.[7] I have signed Exhibits A and B and attached . . . I am the direct supervisor of the employee in question . . .

Events: On August 24 . . . I received information from others that led me to believe that . . . was falsifying travel vouchers . . . we sampled two reimbursements . . . included trips that were falsified . . . meetings on December 7, 2005 . . . January 23, 2006 . . . I told the departmental chair . . . outlined the misuse . . .

reported that there was more in the files . . .
embezzlement . . . he said he'd speak to persons in the dean's office . . . urgent matter . . . I
was required as director . . . to report this to the
USDA/CDSS since funds that were misused
were federal dollars . . .

My knowledge: I had no knowledge of the
employee's personal travel expenses . . . At this
time, I am fully aware of the misconduct . . .
misuse of federal dollars and the embezzlement, I am required to report this to higher
authorities . . .

Recommendations: I recommend an audit
of . . . travel and all purchases at Fry's Electronics . . . I expect the funds to be returned to
the program budget and I strongly recommend
that she be terminated by the appropriate process on Monday, August 28, 2006.

Signed Amy Block Joy, Director

I included copies of the university's official forms to report
crime: Whistleblower Exhibits A (whistleblower cover page)
and B (retaliation protection document). Fred couldn't say I
was out of step with the university!

I spent some time considering all the possible ways to file
my report. I believed that the right thing to do was to file
the report openly, using my name and title. The policy did
provide scope for anonymous reporting and even provided
ways to do so. However, besides my imploding need to follow an ethical code, I felt that as director of the program
and as a university employee, it was my duty, in fact, my
obligation, to report my allegations unencumbered by being
anonymous. My decision, therefore, was to report the allegations using my name and title and to identify clearly that
this whistleblower report was not anonymous.

My real concern was *whom* to send my report to. My previous attempts at reporting had fallen on deaf ears.

At ten-thirty in the morning I drove through an early morning fog to the main Berkeley post office and threw the letters into the mailbox! As I watched them disappear into a dark hole, I was startled by the blaring of a car alarm behind me. Reporting this to the wrong person was too dangerous. Everyone must know. I mailed copies of my report to the college dean, the executive dean, the associate dean, the director of human resources, Raymond, and Fred. Afraid of sending the report directly to the chancellor, I addressed the envelope, "Chancellor's Office," hoping it would find its way to the right person.

I returned home. The Berkeley fog was lifting as the sun peaked through an almost cloudless sky. I felt a great sense of relief and satisfaction, but even more so, of strength and power.

At 6:15 p.m. the telephone rang.

"Hello," I answered.

"Fred, here, I hope you've calmed down," he began. "You'll need to wait a bit longer," he spoke rapidly. "Raymond and I will meet with Beverly on Wednesday and then . . ."

"Too late," I interrupted him. "I already mailed a whistleblower report to the chancellor!" My heart was pounding as I waited for him to catch his breath.

"The chancellor?" He stopped, his voice incredulous and alarmed. Sheepishly, he asked me what I'd sent.

"Everything," I replied in one word. "I've sent the chancellor everything!"

He was silent. Feeling confident and inspired, I couldn't help but dig in.

"Fred," I continued more calmly, "you and Raymond should get your copy on Tuesday, in time for your meeting with Beverly."

He quickly said good-bye and we hung up. Unfortunately, my confidence and inspiration didn't last very long.

I drove to a friend's house and learned to play Mah Jongg

with four of my closest female buddies. Surprisingly complex and challenging, I concentrated on following the rules and won the first round! I believed this was a good omen, and I felt like a winner. I looked around at the faces of my friends, trying to picture their surprise if I told them my news: I'm a whistleblower.

On Sunday afternoon at about one-thirty I sent Fred a confidential email asking again to put Beverly on paid leave. I was concerned that she'd tamper with evidence and reminded him that the travel fraud was remarkably extensive for a person who was supposed to be sitting at Davis working on a computer.

Fred didn't reply. Instead he sent a two-page email to several officials at UC Davis at two in the afternoon. His email provided background to the dean's office, specifically Associate Dean Percival Grossman, or Percy, as we all called him.

Because Fred didn't know exactly what I'd mailed or even what I wrote in my whistleblower report, his email contained all sorts of rambling information, some of it benign, some of it outright strange. In fact, some of it was revealing. By not telling Fred what I'd sent, it seems I had made him suddenly very anxious to tell his side of the story!

"On Friday, August 26, 2006, Dr. Amy Joy . . . presented evidence that her employee, Beverly . . . has continued to engage in practices that may be described as . . . embezzlement."

Interesting, I said to myself, he used the word "continued." Does this mean he'd already told the dean's office?

Fred also wrote that my evidence had some "ambiguities which cloud determining the extent and range of the charges . . ." *Hmm, what ambiguities?*

Fred then indicated that Beverly was conducting business "on behalf of the department to fulfill obligations associated with a USDA audit . . . and at the bequest of department personnel . . ." *What obligations?*

At the end of the email he provided his own assessment of Beverly. "Ms. Benford was warned by the department that her extensive travel looked suspicious . . . 2004 . . . My personal interactions with Beverly have not been as positive as others (. . . many like her). She has lied to me. I find her obfuscatory and arrogant." Now this was pure Fred, no question about it!

Fred's email concluded, "My recommendations . . . Put Ms. Benford on . . . some sort of administrative leave . . . immediately . . . Accordingly, I would like this settled in a way that is removed from direct department involvement . . . if fraud has been committed it has to be dealt with but I hope . . . not compromise . . . some important . . . colleagues."

I called Dean Grossman and left a message at his home. He replied by emailing his schedule. He had a tennis game and a visit to his daughter and indicated that he'd not get my letter until Tuesday. He said that Fred had called him on Friday.

Considering that Fred had already "let the cat out of the bag," I sent Percy an email with my whistleblower report attached so he wouldn't have to wait until Tuesday to take action. I was still worried that Beverly would destroy evidence.

I sent another email about protecting the evidence to everyone on Fred's list.

I prepared a draft to put Beverly on administrative leave first thing Monday morning. However, Percy wrote me an email, asking me to take a step back.

"I would be somewhat more collegial than your proposed note conveys . . . there is nothing wrong with showing compassion for someone . . . your relationship with Beverly has much emotion . . . warm and hot . . ."

I couldn't help but wonder what Fred had told him.

On Monday, August 28, 2006, I arrived at Davis at six-thirty in the morning, ready to face Beverly. Percy asked me to meet with Shirley Handover, director of human resources, at seven-thirty. I called Shirley, and she listened intently, provided rudimentary instructions, and sent me a letter to give to Beverly. I was to put Beverly on an "investigatory leave," collect all her keys and her Blackberry, and have her sign a "proof of service."

I went upstairs to get a list of her keys from the office receptionist, a new temporary employee and the only person in that usually buzzing office. Raymond and Fred hadn't arrived.

The key list wasn't correct. My office key that unlocked everything wasn't listed. Beverly frequently used her copy to get into my office. I called Shirley, who said to only collect the keys on the list. *Who gave Beverly a copy of my key?*

At eight o'clock I found April Jefferson, the departmental management service officer (MSO), in her office and asked her if she'd be available to be a witness to the leave notification. I also asked another staff member, Jerry Fields, to accompany us and be a second witness. Jerry was a nice guy, tall and a bit gawky, and he knew Beverly. I hoped having him there would provide some level of comfort to Beverly. April on the other hand, very smart and even-tempered, had never met Beverly. I told both of them that Beverly was being put on a short-term investigatory leave and that I was concerned that she might make a dramatic exit. I had already called all my staff and asked them not to come to work until the afternoon. I made it clear that they shouldn't tell Beverly I had called them.

April and Jerry waited in my office while I went next door to see if Beverly had arrived. Jerry was very nervous. I saw Beverly pouring herself a cup of coffee in the room next to her office. Her back was turned, and I quickly went to get April and Jerry. They followed me into the room where Beverly was standing. The time was 8:15 a.m.

Beverly was stirring her coffee when we walked in. I said a curt hi and asked her to take a seat.

"Beverly, I need to talk to you about a serious issue."

She glared at me.

"You know April and Jerry," I continued as she stared at them. "Please have a seat. I want you to read a letter."

I handed her the letter. She continued to stand, after putting her coffee on the desk. She then slowly took the letter.

> Subject: Letter of Investigatory Leave
> Dear Ms. Benford:
>
> This letter confirms that you are being
> placed on paid investigatory leave effective
> today, Monday, August 28, 2006. You are
> hereby relieved immediately from all work
> duties . . . I anticipate the investigation will run
> . . . two to three weeks.
> You must remain available during normal
> business hours to participate in this investiga-
> tion . . .
> If you have questions . . . contact campus
> Employee Relations Office . . . regarding your
> rights . . .
>
> Sincerely,
> Amy Joy

She read the letter quickly, then immediately started speaking as she tried to hand the letter back to me.

"Where's Raymond?" she asked quite assertively. "I need to
talk to him." She was growling at me.

"Beverly," I quickly responded, "there is a telephone number to call with questions. In the meantime, I need to help you
gather up any personal belongings you want to take with you."
She was staring at the closed door, and I wondered if she'd run
upstairs to find Raymond.

After a brief pause, I continued. "I also need to get your keys.
I have a list of the keys from upstairs. We need to go over the
list together and fill out this proof of service form."

She pushed the paper I was trying to show her.

"I need to speak to Raymond, now," she repeated. "Is he
upstairs?"

I ignored her question and asked her to step inside her office.
I asked Jerry to get a box for her. He put one on her chair.

"Beverly, please give me your seven keys and your Blackberry."
I looked at the clock and noted the time on the service paper. It
was almost 8:30 a.m.

She took her time looking for her keys and her Blackberry in
her purse. She took out her Blackberry and put it on her desk,
then put a lot of clutter from her purse on top of it. She then
found her key chain and sat down on her chair, taking a lot of
time trying to remove the office keys from the key chain. She
had about twenty-five keys on the chain and removing each one
took several minutes. She used a large letter opener to pry the
keys off the chain. I matched the key number with the list and
checked each key, noting it on the proof of service form.

Suddenly her Blackberry was no longer on her desk. She
had somehow managed to put it back into her purse! I asked
for her Blackberry again. She bent down under the desk to pull
it out of her purse again, and remained there trying to use it.
I asked her to get up and then took the Blackberry from her.
She'd turned it on; I saw the name Savage on the screen as I
turned it off.

She then went through the stacks of stuff on her desk. She'd
put her assortment of teas and coffee mugs in the box. Next she
started going through post-its on her desk. I let her do this for
a few minutes, then suggested she might want to put her desk
photos in the box.

"Just personal belongings," I said trying to get her attention.
"Shall we help you with the desk photos?"

"Those are staying," she said grimly and left them on her desk.

"How about your tennis shoes?"

"Those are staying, too. I'll be back."

She asked again for Raymond and repeated her request to
talk to him. I didn't respond. She got choked up when she said
his name, but she didn't shed a tear.

I asked her to open her cabinets. She flashed an angry look at
me but opened them.

"You just wait," she said threateningly as she opened the locked drawer with a key from her key ring. After she opened it, I asked for the key. She again spent a few minutes removing it from her key chain. It was now 9:10 a.m.

There was a box of keys in the drawer.

"Are these the keys to the files?" She nodded and clumsily shoved the box into my hands, making some of the keys spill onto the floor. Jerry got on his hands and knees and gathered them up.

Opening her desk drawer with the key, she removed a handful of files and started to put them in her box to take home. I noticed that one of the files was bright red. "Beverly, you're not allowed to take any work-related items from the office," I said in the firmest voice I could muster.

"These are my personal files. See," she insisted, showing me her performance evaluations. "These don't belong to UC. They're mine and I'm taking them."

"Nevertheless," I began, thinking quickly, "we need to make copies of them to send to you later." I took them out of the box. She tried to grab them from me. Suddenly aware that her behavior indicated that something was very amiss, I repeated myself even more assertively.

"You may not take any office files with you, only your personal belongings. I'll make a note that you'd like copies sent to you." I held tightly onto the red file and wrote a note on the proof of service form.

I quickly opened the folder to glance inside. I couldn't believe what I was seeing: the first page was covered in my signature in red ink. *She had been practicing signing my name!*

Frightened by how easily I could have been fooled into letting her take this home, I handed the file to April, showed her the page where my signature had been practiced, and asked her to put it in a bag for safekeeping.

Beverly began to protest again, this time more vocally.

"I know my rights. Give me back my files. This is wrong. You can't do this to me. Just you wait . . ." Her lip was curling now.

"Human resources will send you a copy. April will be tak-ing the folder to them right away." April displayed no emotion whatsoever. I could see that Jerry was getting anxious.

I removed all the files from Beverly's box and told her that she needed to finish up.

"Beverly, it's now 9:15 a.m. and time to go."

She seemed stressed, and I suddenly feared she would snap. She said she needed water, pushed me aside, and walked over to get a drink from our water dispenser. I followed her like a hawk. I didn't notice that she'd picked up something from her desk and walked straight to the shredder. She put in the two-page document. Right on her heels, I pulled it out. It was mostly trash by the time I got there. I unplugged the machine before the rest was gobbled up. On her way back to her office, she got herself a cup of water.

I asked Beverly what she shredded.

"Just an old travel voucher."

"Was it for your travel?"

"No, like I said an old document. Nothing to bother about," she said flippantly.

"You need to finish up your packing," I told her. "No more shredding of documents, old or new." She finished at 9:30 a.m. She and I both signed the proof of service about the keys, and I gave her a copy. Jerry carried the box and escorted her to her car according to my strict "no detour" instructions. They left at 9:40 a.m.

I asked April to take the files that Beverly wanted to keep to the dean's office. I was very curious to see what they contained.

I then checked the keys to see if any of them fit my door. None of them worked. I knew she had my key—which opened the building, my office, and her office—and was sure that meant she'd be back. When I tried to lock her desk drawer with the cabinet key she gave me, it didn't work, either. In fact, the box of cabinet keys that she'd produced didn't unlock anything!

She had not given me the key she used. Her key chain had so many keys on it and I hadn't checked to make sure that the key she handed me fit the lock. It didn't. I used duct tape to secure all her drawers tightly. At least I'd know if she tried to get into them again.

I wrote up what happened and sent it to Shirley for the record. Jerry returned and said that he'd seen her off in her car. He said she drove out of the parking lot and turned right instead of left. This meant that she didn't go to the freeway and home. Jerry also said that he saw her turn on her cell phone as she drove away. He sounded quite shaken.

Suspecting she was talking to Raymond, I went upstairs and was told that he was working at home all day. Fred hadn't yet arrived. He was expected in the afternoon.

I went to the dean's office to meet with Shirley so I could look more closely at the page in the red file. Both Shirley and I studied it. Clearly, she was practicing signing my name.

Also in the file were blank leave records, blank purchase orders, and a copy of my real signature on a document. I swallowed hard—her practiced forgery of my signature was pretty damn good!

I went upstairs and found Fred sitting at his desk working on his computer. I wanted his approval to have the locks changed.

"Hi Fred," I said cheerfully, "you missed an exciting morning." Fred seemed quiet and pensive.

"Is Raymond around?" I asked, trying to sound more serious.

"He's out of town," Fred answered.

I expected he'd ask me about Beverly. He didn't.

"This morning I put Beverly on leave and . . . " I began.

Fred got very defensive. "She's quite distressed about all this!" I was taken aback.

"Did you speak to her over the weekend?" I asked, recalling that she didn't seem too surprised when I gave her the letter.

"I'm allowed to talk to her," he said angrily. "I didn't speak to her directly, someone else did. You know that she's very popular in the department," he said, looking annoyed. He was really steaming now. "These are only allegations and nothing has been proven. She's allowed to get help from folks here. Raymond's concerned about her."

"Did Raymond talk to her?"

"Raymond's gullible," Fred said matter-of-factly. "Anyway, it's out of our hands now," he said glaring at me. "Raymond feels that innocent people will be hurt by all this . . . " His voice trailed off as he lowered his head.

"Innocent?" I asked. "Do you believe Beverly is innocent?"

He didn't answer. At the mention of Beverly his usual jolly face wrinkled with disgust.

After that conversation with Fred, I telephoned Shirley and requested that the locks on all our offices be changed. I explained that Beverly had a copy of my key, which opened all the offices. I was told that an order would be put in. Much to my dismay, no locksmith arrived.

I took everything that I thought might be evidence and put it in the trunk of my car for safekeeping. Then I labeled the remaining boxes in my office in large, black letters "Confidential" and "Investigation" and stuck a random assortment of papers into them. I even labeled some files "Beverly Benford" and pulled out stuff from the recycle bin, packing the boxes full.

If someone did come into my office, they'd have a lot of work sorting through these dummy boxes. I hid the shredder.

Before going home, I waited for the custodian to empty the wastebaskets, then placed transparent tape on all the doors toward the bottom where it was less likely to be seen. I also left small pieces of numbered paper on each of the boxes in my office. If any box was opened, I would find the paper on the floor, and then I'd know which one it was.

Just before going home, I drew a picture of Beverly's desk area and catalogued everything on it, by stack location and description. I'd know if things were disturbed. I left for home at nine in the evening. On my way, I wondered why the dean's office hadn't come over and sealed the scene with yellow tape. I thought embezzlement was a crime!

When I arrived the next day at six-thirty in the morning, I saw the broken tape on the doors to both my and Beverly's offices. Someone had clearly been there during the night.

Then I looked in my office. All the numbered pieces of paper were on the floor, and my boxes were scattered everywhere. In fact, many of the files were placed back in the box backwards. The same was true for Beverly's desk. Although things on her desk had been moved and rearranged, nothing was actually missing.

The duct-taped cabinets had not been disturbed.

I sent an email to human resource director Shirley Handover about my office being ransacked. She never replied.

Obviously, nobody was getting the picture! I called Shirley; her assistant was very friendly, but not very helpful; she said she'd give Shirley the message.

That was the second night I went home exhausted.

On day three, Ginny told me that Beverly had left her a phone message on her home machine. "Beverly said you filed a whistleblower report against her," she told me that morning. "Beverly said, 'Amy will be sorry she messed with me.'" I reassured Ginny that she wasn't identified in my whistleblower report. Beverly's phone call was reported to human resources and later in the week Ginny received some guidance, although she decided that she just wasn't going to answer her telephone.

Toward the end of the week I heard from Fred, who copied me on an email he sent to Raymond about a situation on the Berkeley campus. An assistant chancellor had been accused of misuse of university funds. The amount was $2,000. Fred's email was odd. He wrote, "If an Assistant Chancellor has to go to the police for $2,000, please be careful." I noticed that his email was sent only to me and Raymond.

On Friday, September 1, I received a phone call about meeting with the internal audit department on the Tuesday after Labor Day. The auditors had requested an hour. I called back and suggested to their administrative assistant that I thought we might need two hours.

Greatly relieved, I believed I'd give them the evidence boxes and get on with my life. Little did I know what was in store for me!

All day Saturday I prepared for my meeting with the auditors. I assembled in chronological order a file box with all the letters, telephone call notes, meeting notes, documents, and my report and attachments.

As proof that the two-month travel audit had turned up fabricated trips, I printed emails that showed Beverly was sitting at her computer in Davis and was not on the road or attending meetings. I created a timeline and numbered the documents to match the events. I felt very prepared. I copied my forty-page narrative from my desktop computer onto my laptop.

On Sunday, September 3, I received a phone call from Percy. He wanted to see me and asked if he could come over. I thought that he wanted to congratulate me on my whistleblower report. I changed out of my sweats, took a shower, and put on a pantsuit worthy of congratulations.

Percy called again to let me that he wouldn't be over until a little later in the day. He sounded tense, so I asked him if he was okay. He said that his visit was for official university business and that he couldn't talk about it over the telephone. He sounded odd, almost cold, as though he'd forgotten we were friends. I reminded him how to get to my house.

He called a third time, having gotten lost. I gave him another set of instructions because he'd gone into the Berkeley Hills. He called a fourth time to tell me that he was outside my door. I went to the door and he wasn't there. He'd gone to the wrong house!

I came out to find him looking puzzled in our driveway. He'd parked his car halfway down the driveway to my house and mistakenly knocked on the door of my neighbor.

Percy was wearing a white tennis outfit. He looked rather fit and athletic in his white shorts and tennis shoes. I could even picture him swinging the racket as I walked toward him. His wife, also dressed in white and wearing shades, was in the car. I waved at her. She didn't wave back.

He came over to me and handed me a letter. "Oh," I said surprised, "is this letter for me?" I was surprised that he didn't hug me as he usually did when we met.

He then said very stiffly, "Yes, and you need to open it and read it out loud to me."

I flushed with embarrassment, then nervously opened the envelope and pulled out the letter. My heart was pounding, and it was difficult to take in the information. However, I did get the gist of it, and it wasn't good.

> September 1, 2006
> Amy Block Joy: Investigation of Allegations
>
> Dear Dr. Joy:
> I have been informed that a whistleblower report has been filed alleging you engaged in improper business activities at UC Davis. In the coming days, you will receive a letter ... explaining in greater detail ... While the investigation is in progress ... I am directing you to refrain from performing your admin- istrative and management responsibilities ... you should not approve ... not access business, financial, personnel, or administrative files ... These activities will be ... managed by depart- mental chair, Dr. Fred Stone.
>
> Sincerely,
> Percival Grossman, associate dean

"Percy, this must be Beverly!" I gasped. "Isn't there some rule that prohibits her from harassing me?" I asked.

He stood there, unmoved and stiff.

I asked him, "Did you see the evidence and her confession?"

He continued to say nothing, just standing in my driveway in his tennis shorts.

"Isn't it ironic that she's claiming to be a whistleblower?" I tried again to engage him. He stared straight away and avoided looking at me.

Finally he spoke.

"Fred has a different view of things," he said coldly.

"What did he say?"

"I can't talk about it. His meeting with Beverly was confidential."

"Percy," I said trying to get him to look at me, "this letter isn't very specific. The letter doesn't provide the allegations. I have a right to know what the allegations are."

He didn't answer and turned away. He then asked me to sign a proof of service. After I signed it, he got back into his car and he drove off to play tennis.

Needless to say, I was shaken to the core. Of all that I'd read about being a whistleblower, nothing had prepared me for this.

On Tuesday, September 5, I drove straight to the auditor's office. I called Ginny to tell her that I'd arrive in the office late. I didn't mention to anyone that I'd received a letter from the university served to me in my driveway by a dean on his way to play tennis. I was told that my meeting with the auditors was confidential.

The auditor's office was very neatly organized. The room was air-conditioned, and everyone in the office seemed relaxed and low-key. I felt very comfortable and safe in their office. I introduced myself as the whistleblower.

I met with three auditors, two men and a woman. All were very professional. They were quick to make me feel comfortable, asking if I'd like a cup of water and explaining very clearly their interview process.

They had a list of questions but asked me to tell my story first. I began by showing them my box of documents, each one numbered even though I knew every date, time, and event by heart. As I spoke, I pulled supporting evidence out of my box.

Everyone was quiet for the entire ninety minutes it took me to explain what had happened. When I was done, my numbered list had been gone through, and there was a stack of documents in the middle of the table.

I experienced some momentary relief once that initial stage was over. They made copies of all my documents in my plastic box and returned the originals to me. For the next thirty minutes, I answered their questions about my role and Beverly's job at the university. By then, it was almost noon. I then asked about the letter I'd received and the whistleblower allegations against me. One of the auditors left the room, then returned to say that she was allowed to tell me the specific allegations against me, and that I'd get the official letter later in the mail.

Two of the three auditors, Lawrence and Juliet, remained in the room. They asked me if I wanted to take a break before discussing the allegations against me. I told them I was fine, not even tired, and that I preferred to hear everything right away.

There were three allegations against me for "improper governmental activities." I carefully wrote down each one as it was read. They were, indeed, bizarre. I had Lawrence read the sentences a couple of times to make sure I was understanding them correctly.

1. The Director authorized payment of program funds to three individuals who should not have received payments because they are not part of the program and are not included in the program budget.
2. The Director has inappropriately claimed commuting mileage on her TEVs (travel expense vouchers) since October 1, 2005.
3. The Director authorized an employee to claim commuting mileage on TEVs from April 1, 2006 through July 31, 2006.

The first one was so strange I asked the auditors to name the individuals and provide more details. I was accused of making inappropriate payments to Jonnie Tao of San Francisco County and Arturo Romero of Contra Costa County. The third individual working in Santa Clara wasn't named, so that allegation was tossed for being "unsubstantiated."

"I can give preliminary explanations for each of these allegations right now," I replied, "and get you backup documentation soon."

I had tons of emails, work products, and deliverables, including the hard work Jonnie and Arturo had done developing curriculum, handouts, and educational materials for the program. In addition, I had a publication Arturo and I had authored on improved diets in poor families. Beverly was crazy—I had copied her on all those emails!

"I have a box of documents that will give you plenty of proof that these two persons are working for the program and have been for many years." I explained what they did and gave plenty of examples to demonstrate that their work was appropriate.

As for the second allegation, I explained that I had been on sabbatical leave and received advanced approval for reimbursement claims to attend meetings in Sacramento and Davis. I just needed to provide my sabbatical report, and my approval form. That would be easy.

For the third allegation, I told the auditors that I never signed any of the TEVs for the employee in question. The auditors would be able to secure the TEVs from accounts payable and see that Dr. Raymond Savage had signed them, not me.

When I got back to my office, the confidential letter from the chancellor's office was in my mail box. The envelope was addressed to me and contained a letter dated September 5 outlining the whistleblower complaint of "Improper Governmental Activities" against me.

I wondered if Raymond and Fred had told Beverly during their Wednesday off-campus meeting that I'd filed a whistleblower report against her and that was why she had in turn filed one against me. The dates certainly matched my speculation.

Seeing the allegations on paper upset me again. What would happen next, I wondered.

Not being able to go into the offices next door and meet with my staff was disquieting. I was worried that I might be accused of tinkering with the files. Luckily I had always been compulsive about keeping copies of all my work at home, so I'd have no trouble putting together the documentation for my defense.

I kept a low profile at work during the week, hoping that things would settle down to a simmer and that no one would notice that I was stuck in my office and couldn't meet with my staff. I had tons of programmatic work to do to get approval for our $14 million program contract. All administrative and financial emails that I would have sent to the USDA were sent to Fred instead. Fred forwarded the emails to the USDA and copied me.

With Beverly gone, everyone was abuzz with speculations. No one was talking to me about her, though Ginny was constantly filling me in on the gossip.

In between doing my job of securing another year of funding for the program, I worked on my defense, especially at night after returning home from work. On September 7, I finished my official response to the allegations and that afternoon returned to the auditor's office with two boxes of documents to support my claims. In the box were work products from the two employees who reported to me (allegation #1) and my sabbatical report and approval form (allegation #2). The auditors would get the records from accounts payable to document who signed the three TEVs (allegation #3).

That afternoon I was given permission by the head of UCD Internal Audit Services, Stephen Grant, to alert the director of the USDA about the alleged fraud. The next day the director sent me an email indicating that the USDA contacted the Office of the Inspector General (OIG) because the embezzled funds were federal dollars.

The second week of September, things began to calm down. Ginny and I would go get coffee at the Silo Cafe and trade Beverly stories. We didn't discuss the investigation, only our past relationship with Beverly. It was fun getting to know Ginny, and we were both happily surprised at our budding relationship. I found out that Beverly had scheduled Ginny to work on the days that I wasn't in the office, so our paths rarely crossed over the years. Ginny told me sadly that Beverly frequently said that I'd made negative comments about her work. I let Ginny know that Beverly never spoke about her work. Beverly had kept us apart now for five years, and we were making up for lost time!

Initially I was fixated on why Raymond would help Beverly. I was asked repeatedly by the investigators and other officials about whether or not there was some sort of personal relationship between Beverly and Raymond. I figured that if this were true, Ginny would know.

But my indirect approach with Ginny wasn't working, so I had to be careful what she might deduce from any questions I asked her.

On Monday, September 11, 2006, I finally asked Ginny if Beverly ever complained about Raymond.

"Oh, no, no, no," Ginny said shaking her head firmly. "Beverly never complained about Raymond. Just the opposite," Ginny giggled. "It was always, Raymond said this and Raymond said that." She mimicked Beverly.

"Beverly always hinted to me that she and Raymond were close," I said to Ginny, picturing Beverly shaking her two fingers at me.

"Well, as a matter of fact," Ginny began thoughtfully, "Beverly always giggled when she talked about him. It was kind of embarrassing. She had this school-girl crush on him, and I'd tease her about it," Ginny said.

"Ohhh, this sounds interesting," I said. "What would you say?" I asked.

"I'd sing to her in the car on our way home from work," Ginny said, "Beverly loves Raymond, Beverly loves Raymond."

"How would she react?" I asked, picturing a lovesick Beverly.

"Oh, she'd shush me. But then, as she was shushing, she'd

grin and grin. She really liked him, even said he was very attractive, very manly!" Both Ginny and I burst out laughing at the thought.

"Then she'd remind me that he was the famous Dr. Savage and that I shouldn't call him Raymond!"

"So, Ginny," I finally asked, "any shenanigans?"

Ginny smiled broadly. "You know Beverly. She thinks she's above it all! As to the affairs of the heart, she's pretty earthy and not at all shy. I wouldn't put it past her to do her damnedest to get what she wanted."

On Wednesday September 13, I received a message from the UC Davis Police Department, requesting an interview on Thursday. Thinking about Percy's cold demeanor in my driveway, and knowing that Beverly had filed a whistleblower complaint against me, I wondered who'd organized the interview with the police. I was reminded not to talk to anyone. I replied as upbeat as possible, confirming the meeting, although in my heart I was far from upbeat.

Just before going home to prepare for my police interview, I ran up to the third floor to pick up my mail, wondering if I'd find another scary letter in my mailbox. I ran into Fred, who now was the acting director of my program during the investigation.

I was going up and Fred was coming down the stairs. Fred began speaking to me at the top of the second floor. I wasn't quite to the landing when I heard his voice echoing up and down the four-story stairwell.

"I've been looking for you," Fred greeted me with enthusiasm.

"Hey Fred, how are you?" I said grabbing a hold of the metal rail trying to sound chipper. Fred waddled toward me.

He slowly grinned. "I've been wanting to show you something in my office." He was now almost directly in front of me.

"Really?" I was a little curious but very wary.

"I have a stack of purchase orders with your signature." Looking amused at my discomfort, he smiled. It was the kind of smile that a snake might use to greet a helpless wounded furry creature.

"Let's go up and see them," I suggested cheerfully. This might be very useful information for my interview.

"Can't. I'm on my way out." He grunted like a caveman.

"OK, how about tomorrow?" I persisted.

"You signed a lot of purchase orders. I'd say there's about fifty or sixty of them in the stack I have. And according to the account manager, there's a lot more."

"Fifty or sixty!" I was now alarmed. "You must be mistaken." I was quite clear about that! I'd already printed a copy of the inventory list that Beverly prepared for me each year. My estimation was that I signed about five or six each year, mainly for computer purchases. Maybe he was talking about ten years of purchase orders?

"You approved them," he said, trying to make a point. I wasn't sure where he was going.

"Come on, Fred," I insisted, "now you've got me really curious. I want to see that stack."

"Are you telling me she forged your signature?"

Now, startled, I wondered, *Who told Fred that we found evidence of her practicing my signature? What's he suggesting?*

Suddenly feeling like this was some sort of trick, I looked down at my watch. "Oh my god, I'm late. I'll catch up with you later," I said, waving as I ran up the stairs to the third floor.

Only a handful of people knew about the evidence of her practicing my signature. Shirley, Percy, and the auditors were the only ones party to this discovery. *Did Percy tell Fred?*

I called Ginny at home that night and asked her about the purchase order process that Beverly used. I wanted to see if it was different than what she told me, and I was curious why Fred had copies.

"Ginny, sorry to call you at home, but I wanted to ask you about something Dr. Stone mentioned to me today."

"Dr. Stone—this ought to be good!" Ginny was upbeat.

"He said that he had copies of our purchase orders. Do you

think Beverly gave him copies?"

Ginny then explained the whole procedure. She and Tessa prepared the orders for Beverly. They had strict instructions that only Dr. Savage could approve purchases and travel reimbursements.

"Beverly was very specific that only the departmental chair could approve these transactions," Ginny recalled, adding, "or Dr. Stone, if Dr. Savage was out of town."

"And what about me?" I asked dumbfounded.

"Oh, she was very clear about you," Ginny confided. "Beverly said that the departmental chair was the only approving party to purchases and travel, and not to bother you," Ginny told me. "In fact, we were given specific instructions never to leave the purchase orders or travel vouchers in a mailbox. We had to go upstairs and get the signatures personally from Dr. Savage. Beverly was always complaining that papers tended to get lost on the third floor."

"Yes," I sighed, recalling something Beverly told me. "Beverly frequently called them the third-floor dummies! My travel submissions kept getting lost, and I'd frequently have to complete a lost receipt form. Luckily, I made copies of what I submitted to Beverly. Of course, she would tell me several weeks after I submitted my claim that receipts had been lost and my reimbursement would then take a couple of months."

"I know," Ginny said. "Beverly made it clear to all of us to do your travel last. I bet Beverly took your original receipts and used them herself to get travel reimbursement," Ginny guessed suddenly. I was speechless.

"Is this possible? Wouldn't accounts payable notice that two people were using the same receipts?"

Ginny thought about it. "Probably not. With the extra paperwork for lost receipts, the time lag between hers and yours would make it nearly impossible to discover."

Thinking quickly to myself, *no wonder she used my meetings and receipts to fabricate her travel!*

"Whoa—that's pretty sophisticated, even for Beverly.

"Ginny," I continued changing the subject, "back to Dr. Stone.

When I bumped into him he said he had copies of purchase orders. Why would Fred be keeping copies?"

"Let me put on my detective hat," Ginny kidded. "I think Dr. Stone is pulling your leg! He's trying to find out what you know. He doesn't keep purchase orders. He's just fishing for information. He does it to me all the time."

Ginny said that he came down to her office the other day and asked her if she knew about the anti-whistleblower complaint that Beverly filed against me.

"He told you that!" I was shocked. *It must be Beverly!*

"Yes, and he even asked me how you felt about it. However, since you never told me all I could say to him was, 'I don't know.'"

"When did this happen?" I asked Ginny.

"I thought I told you. Last week, I think. Sorry, too much is going on," she sighed, indicating that she was a little tired of all the excitement. "What's an anti-whistleblower complaint?"

"Oh, it's Dr. Stone's way of telling me that I need to watch out for Beverly!" I tried to make light of it. "Did he say anything else?"

Ginny thought and said that was it.

"But he'll be back. He likes our cookies! Dr. Stone's so funny. He plops down in the chair next to me and talks to me as though we're old buddies. He's my best source of information about Beverly!" Ginny and I both laughed at the irony.

I made a mental note that Fred called it an anti-whistleblower complaint. This was actually very revealing because it indicated that the person who filed it was, indeed, Beverly. However, Fred wasn't supposed to tell anyone about the whistleblower complaint against me—this could be considered a breach. I called the auditors to let them know that Ginny had been told. As was their custom, they never confirmed nor denied Fred's assertion.

I got up very early that September morning and looked through my closet, wondering what I should wear to the police station. I selected my navy blue Jones of New York pinstripe suit. The weather was cold in the Bay Area due to the early morning fog. I usually found that Davis was much hotter, although with air-conditioning, offices tended to be very cold.

I was confused by the unfolding of events from one day to the next. And I wasn't sure who arranged for the police interview. By now, I was constantly on guard, and the stress was wearing me down.

I picked up my audit box to bring with me and drove to Davis early that morning. Before the interview, I stopped off at the office to say hello to Ginny, who by now was pretty much the only person I trusted.

I asked Ginny to come into my office; I still wasn't allowed into our main offices because of the allegations against me.

Ginny greeted me with, "Whoa, you're lookin' good today in your jailhouse stripes. Where ya goin'?" I was taken aback.

Did I communicate unconsciously to her that I had a police interview?

"You know me, Ginny," I joked. "This is my lucky suit. It's the same suit I wore on Beverly's last day!" In fact, in one of my pockets I found a bunch of little numbered slips of paper, the ones I found on the floor in my ransacked office.

I printed the email interview request with the address of the police station and hurried to my car, wondering what was going to happen next.

6 | Trauma

I entered the police station office and asked for Lieutenant Detective Jonathan Goodman. The police receptionist led me to the interview room and opened the door for me. The room was empty; I took a seat facing the door and waited.

Lieutenant Detective Goodman walked in, took a seat across from me, and began filling out some forms. He introduced me to another detective, who had been chatting with him in the hallway.

"This is Detective Damien Cruz," he said. The tall uniformed police officer smiled. His eyes were friendly, and he reminded me of a policeman I had met many years before. I was introduced to a third police officer as he quietly entered the room and sat down.

Ready to face the truth, I spent almost two hours talking about my March 2 confrontation with Beverly, and the evidence I had collected regarding the embezzlement. It was a relief to finally talk about it. They had my letter and Beverly's response. The police listened intently but the minute I mentioned Dr. Raymond Savage, they zeroed in. They seemed much more interested in Raymond than Beverly. *Had Raymond been interviewed? I was too nervous to ask.*

My mind started buzzing when they asked relationship questions about Raymond. *Why was Raymond protecting Beverly? What should I say if they ask me?*

I answered all their questions while my mind was spinning

trying to make sense of everything.

If Raymond had approved Beverly's transactions and was sign-
ing them, why did he act like he didn't know anything and then
give me such a hard time about it? What was he hiding? Was he
involved? Covering it up?

And what about Fred? Why didn't he want to immediately report
the crime? It took two hours for me to reach the conclusion that
was probably clear in the minds of the police right from the
start: that Raymond was in big trouble. The chatty one, Detective Cruz, smiled at me. "You must feel a big sense of relief now
that your ordeal is over," he said as he walked to the door.

Suddenly alone in the room and feeling cold from sitting so
long, I shivered as I flashed back on an event in my childhood
of getting rescued by a friendly police officer. I hadn't thought
about that rescue, and that trauma, for a long, long time.

In the summer of 1962, when I was nine years old, my father
had dropped me off near the beach at Carmel, California. In the
distance, I could see the ocean sparkling on that bright sunny day.

"I'll pick you up at three o'clock at the entrance to the beach.
Don't be late," he warned me as I stepped out of the idling car
onto the asphalt.

I stood on the side of the road with a towel rolled up under my
arm and fixed my pink Minnie Mouse watch that had slid around
to the wrong side of my wrist. The time was exactly one o'clock.

My father hadn't even turned off the engine of our '60 four-
door Pontiac Bonneville when he slowed and suddenly pulled
over. We were far from the sidewalk, but he insisted that the
beach was close. I was sitting in the back seat and as I reached
to open the door, he put the car into park with his foot firmly
on the brake.

"There it is." His voice was dry and flat, his mind preoccupied
with something else. His fingers were tapping on the steering wheel,
indicating a nervous impatience for me to get out of the car.

As I shut the car door, I turned to wave good-bye. He wasn't
looking at me. His head was turned, and I guessed he was con-

centrating on how to make a U-turn from the middle of the
street. Feeling the warm sun on my forehead, I turned around
and watched the car disappear.

My father, Sy, my mother, Ruthie, and I had arrived a few
minutes before this in Carmel, California, pulling up in front of
a fancy French restaurant. Mother wanted to do some shopping
after lunch but my father wanted to leave by three in order to
avoid what he called "a traffic nightmare."

"Who cares about the traffic?" She was prickly and exasper-
ated. They had promised me I could go to the beach all the way
down to Carmel.

"You promised . . . " I protested, but no one was listening. I
didn't want to eat lunch at that boring fancy restaurant, so I
said, "Can I go to the beach while you eat?"

I wanted to find shells and build a sand castle. The smell of
the ocean and the temptation of the warm sand filled me with
anticipation. I could hardly wait to get my feet wet as I imagined myself walking along the beach's edge.

In response to my question, my mother had slammed the
door shut again as she remained in the passenger seat, furious
at my father for getting lost, not asking directions to the restaurant, and then taking so long to find it. She quickly put on fresh
lipstick before stepping out of the car.

"Sy, you take her to the beach while I get a table."

Starting off on my beach adventure, I stepped over to the
sidewalk and then skipped happily all the way to the bottom of
the hill. The walkway was very clean, and the light on the ocean
was hypnotic. The street was strangely empty, and there were no
traffic lights, so I reached the bottom quite quickly.

At the bottom, however, the sidewalk ended abruptly. A sign
was posted, "No Entrance to Beach." Tall bushes and weeds
lined a small field, and a wooden fence blocked the view. I
turned left and continued. The road curved a bit downward,
and the sidewalk ended a short distance from the sign. From
there on, the ground was uneven and some of it wasn't paved.

This new path was lined with tall shady trees, automotive shops, broken-down cars, and some dilapidated vacant homes. Front yards were full of weeds with warning signs that read, "Private Property—Do Not Enter."

My mind was totally absorbed imagining the sandy beach, so I wasn't aware of how long I spent walking on this path before I reached another street. I could smell the ocean, but I couldn't see it. The road turned toward the right, curved around a long shaded corner, and finally, there was the beach! It was magnificent!

I found a stick and a rusty can. I even found a paper bag to put the stuff in I encountered along the way. At the beach entrance, I took off my flip-flops to feel the warm sand on my feet.

I don't remember seeing anyone on the beach, though I do remember a couple of sandy dogs who came over to sniff the kelp that I had pulled out of the ocean to line my castle moat. I looked for shells to make a sand castle near the water's edge. The time went by quickly, and soon it was time to go. I was completely sandy, but it was too late to clean up. I picked up my shells, shook the sand off the towel, and started on my return trip.

I ran quickly to get there before three, arriving panting and sweaty and with my heart pounding. I thought my mother would be disgusted by my sandy appearance, but I didn't want to make her mad by being late. The entrance was marked by a large rock.

At three o'clock, I was mostly sand-free as I leaned on the rock and wiped the sweat off my face. There was no shade, and my skin was already getting pink from the two hours I'd spent in the sun.

For the first hour, I counted only two cars on the road. *Where was he?* I wondered. I was now feeling hot from the sun, thirsty, and my arm was getting sore from shielding my eyes as I kept watch for my father's car.

At four-thirty I decided to stand on the rock to get a better view. Maybe my father had parked the car and couldn't see me from his parking spot

I could see and hear each car passing from my perch on the rock—the red Mustang with the two blond college boys, their hands with cigarettes loosely dangling out the window. A fast motorcycle skidded sharply as it passed their car. The boys honked back and sped away. Startled by the sudden activity, I was feeling alarmed, as it was now almost five o'clock. My father was going to hit traffic, and it was going to be my fault that they would be unhappy all the way home.

A tall policeman with a bicycle walked over to ask me if I was okay. I said, "Yes, officer, I am waiting for my father to pick me up." I was afraid to tell him that I was worried because my father was now two hours late. My mother had taught me to keep my mouth shut. She often said, "Nobody wants to know how you feel. Children should be seen and not heard." He smiled, waved at me, got back on his bicycle, and pedaled off down the road.

I began to check the time every minute and was beginning to feel panicky. I wondered if I had not heard my father correctly. Maybe I hadn't been paying attention.

The sun was now low and no longer bothering me. I started humming my dad's favorite song while I waited. Hearing the words made me feel comforted and not so alone: *Moon River, wider than a mile, I'm crossing you in style some day. Oh, dream maker, you heart breaker, wherever you're going, I'm going your way* . . . [8] In fact, I was so engaged with the humming, looking, and counting that time passed quickly, and before I knew it, it was after seven. I saw a man on a bicycle coming toward me, but I was afraid and sank back against the rock so he wouldn't see me.

At eight, the sun was setting. I was now using the towel to cover me because it was getting cold and breezy. No cars at all had passed by from six to eight, and the road was unlit. I began to worry that something had happened to my parents. Did they have a car accident?

After the darkness filled the sky, everything slowed then stopped. I stared into the darkness without feeling anything. The splashing of the ocean became quiet, and the buzz of the night bugs dulled. The taste of salt dried up as my tongue grew dry, and my body felt lifeless.

The policeman returned in a police car. Later I was told that it was after nine at night. He shined his light on my face. I was glued to the rock, my head in my hands, cold and speechless. He asked me gently if I was Amy Block. I was unable to respond, my head heavy from the weight of despair. My lips were badly chapped from the wind and sea breeze. He spoke to me very quietly.

"Your parents are at the police station. It's not far from here and I'm going to take you to them."

He was speaking very slowly and softly, with a deep soothing voice.

"You must be very cold. My car is warm. Hold on. I'll get you back to your folks real soon."

Then he picked me up off the rock. I was frozen and stiff from the cold and in the dark I was unable to move my head, see the ground, or even feel my feet. One of my flip-flops had fallen off a while ago. The policeman looked around with his flashlight and found it. He carried me to his car and put me in the seat. He got a blanket from the trunk and covered me, as I was now shivering from the cold.

He chatted to me the entire ride to the station. He said that my father had reported that I was supposed to have met him at the beach entrance. He filed a missing child report about six o'clock after no one at the beach could say they had seen me. He told me that he'd heard a description of me on his police radio and had remembered seeing me sitting on the rock at a completely different street.

He said, "You must have walked a long way."

On the ride to the station, the officer spent a lot of time on his walkie-talkie. I couldn't follow since the words all meshed together into a police code. The warmth of his deep voice was calming, and occasionally he'd turn his head toward me and smile. I managed to look up at him, my face burned by the sun and the wind, and smile back.

"You're going to be feeling good real soon," he said calmly.

When we arrived in the station, he let me stay in his warm car while he used his radio phone to call for my parents to come outside. My eyes didn't like the bright light of the station, and I was still cold and shivering.

I don't recall much after my rescue. I was told that my parents took me to Blums for a hot fudge sundae and that I was much too excited to eat and could hardly sit still in the chair. I wasn't able to let go of my father and clung to him with great joy, relieved that my ordeal was over.

The police returned fifteen minutes later. By this time my eyes were still moist, but I was feeling better. Detective Cruz brought me a cup of water. The three of them thanked me for my help in the investigation. They each shook my hand.

"You've done a courageous thing for the university," he whispered to me.

"Thank you," I said choking back my tears of gratitude.

On Monday morning, September 18, I knocked on Fred's door.

"Come in," I heard Fred say.

"I'd like to see the purchase orders you told me about," I said firmly.

He was sitting at his desk and got up and went to his cabinet.

Leaning on his door, I waited. He opened his cabinet, looked in, and started moving things around as though he was looking for something.

I walked into his office to peak inside his cabinet. I saw a bunch of stuff, mostly journals and clutter.

"Too much stuff in here," he said, looking embarrassed. "You'll have to come back," he finished. I was staring into the cabinet as he held the door open.

"I don't see any purchase orders," I said confidently and turned to face him. "You must have been mistaken."

I walked out of his office. This time he hadn't fooled me with his cat-and-mouse game.

Our program contract deadline was September 29. The renewal process was complicated because the extent of the fraud wasn't clear. Throughout September, I received numerous questions from the USDA, and with fraud hovering in the background, it was challenging to answer their questions. Our responses to their questions were reviewed by the dean's office and then approved by Fred.

However, parts of the budget that Beverly had prepared over the summer were puzzling. To keep things afloat, I put questionable items into a budget amendment, a fancy label for funds that couldn't be justified and would be scrutinized later. The name "Dr. Savage" stuck out like a sore thumb on Beverly's summer spreadsheet. I promptly turned it over to the auditors for review, letting Fred know that some questions just couldn't be answered in time. The rest of the program was approved on September 29, 2006, for approximately $13 million. I breathed a sigh of relief, knowing that the program would continue.

Raymond wasn't around much, and I heard from Fred that he was overseas. I was relieved not to have to bump into him in the hall or mail room. It appeared that he hadn't been interviewed by anyone—but of course my source of information was Fred, and I was very careful not to raise red flags with Fred by asking too many questions.

On October 4, the auditors told me that all the allegations against me were unsubstantiated, and I'd soon receive an official letter that I was cleared. A meeting was arranged that day to make some sort of announcement, although I wasn't invited to attend.

On Thursday, October 5, I asked Ginny if Dr. Stone had mentioned a meeting where an announcement was made about me. I was really curious how they were going to announce that I had been cleared of a bunch of highly confidential allegations.

"You bet," she said shyly. "Fred's been down here talking up a storm about the 'three deans.'"

"The three deans? Is this supposed to be a reference to the Three Tenors?" I asked.

"Well, if it is, then Dr. Stone's singing like a bird," she said laughing.

"He said that three deans came over yesterday and announced

that you were cleared of all charges," Ginny said.

"Wow!" I smiled. "That's definitely good news!"

"According to Dr. Stone, when the announcement was made that you were cleared, everyone in the room tried to look pleased. When someone asked what you were charged with, Dean Percival Grossman said that 'it' was confidential and he wasn't able to comment.

"Dr. Stone asked me if I knew what 'it' was. Then, of course he had to tell me—the anti-whistleblower allegations! He thought the whole thing was really funny. He said, 'Imagine hearing that someone is cleared but no one will admit what they were cleared of,'" Ginny said, quoting Fred.

"Imagine that," I agreed laughing.

On October 18, two federal agents arrived at Davis. I reviewed all the purchase orders from 1998 to 2006 and met with them for several afternoons until the end of October to discuss every purchase made for the program

The two agents were young, very smart and professional. They dressed casually, though they showed me their official badges when we met. As I sat in the room with them, I felt a profound sense of gratitude that the university was doing the right thing. I was proud and honored to be an employee at UC Davis.

I reviewed about four hundred purchase orders that were found at Davis. The copies I reviewed didn't have signatures on them, although they did include the name of the purchaser. Most of them were ordered by Beverly, but I noted other names as well, including my colleague Darci Small. Although I wasn't asked, I was able to easily recall the orders I'd approved as far back as 1998. Some were for legitimate program expenses like office supplies, educational materials, computers, and printers. Most of the four hundred were not. The camcorders, iPods, expensive TVs, stereos, palm pilots, and other electronic goods were not appropriate for our program. It was strange reviewing invoices I'd never seen before. Some items were just plain incomprehensible, like the weird video surveillance system that was ordered in several different batches throughout 2005 and labeled "for El Dorado County."

For two weeks, I answered numerous questions about each of the orders and wrote my answers at the top of each page. The work was completed on the Friday afternoon before Halloween.

The following Monday morning, I received a phone call that informed me that early in the morning on Monday, October 30, 2006, a warrant was served at Beverly's home in Sacramento. Her house was searched and a lot of the electronic goods and equipment were recovered.

I was given permission to tell my staff. We were all shocked! I'd never been to Beverly's home, and Ginny again surprised me with an interesting tidbit.

"I'm picturing the feds walking up the path to Beverly's house, and she's watching them arrive on the video system in her kitchen," Ginny told me. "Did you know she had a very expensive night vision surveillance system installed in her home?" she asked.

"You don't say?" I answered innocently.

"Did you see the system?" I asked.

"Oh yes, everyone who came to her house saw the cameras perched on the roof of her garage and by the front door," Ginny reported. "The video player was installed in her kitchen."

"I'd never been invited to her home," I said, now wondering if this was the reason.

I didn't tell Ginny that this system was part of the stolen property that Beverly purchased in bits and pieces, and that it had cost an arm and a leg.

I felt elated and satisfied. Now that she was caught red-handed, justice would prevail. However, since she wasn't arrested, I imagined she'd be pretty angry, and most likely at me. This made me nervous.

Soon afterward, my car was vandalized in the UCD parking lot. The university worked with the police and a report was filed. There were plenty of people mad at me, so I had no idea who was responsible.

I asked Ginny to call campus services and have the locks of our offices changed immediately since nothing happened after my first request back on August 28. A locksmith arrived and completed the work that afternoon. All my evidence boxes were moved out of my car and into my now secured office.

Fred sent several emails to members of the department about the warrant. Everyone walked around looking stunned and shattered. Many believed that she'd only taken a couple of pieces of equipment. People had been very forgiving of Beverly until now. Everyone now understood that the embezzlement was much more extensive.

On November 1, I received a copy of her resignation letter that she'd addressed to Raymond. The theft estimation, according to Fred and spread via the rumor mill, increased to sixty thousand dollars. This was three times greater than my estimation of twenty thousand on August 24. I wondered if Fred would remember his and Raymond's estimation of two thousand dollars on the same day.

I also heard through the grapevine that Beverly had collected a hefty sum from her UC retirement pension. Ginny and I estimated the one-time payment amount to be about $250,000, based on Beverly's salary and her fourteen years of employment at UC. Unfortunately, none of this money could be touched by the justice system, even though she was under investigation for embezzlement.

I expected that my colleagues would appreciate my work on getting the fraud and theft discovered and corrected and that the need for me to be silent and circumspect would finally be over. I thought that the people who had been friends before the investigation would now return to encircle and support me.

I was wrong.

7 | Retaliation

Late afternoon on Thursday, November 2, I received an email alert from the locally designated official (LDO) for whistleblowers, Assistant Executive Vice-Chancellor Franklin Taylor-Starr, the UC Davis official in charge of the investigation.

I printed the email and dashed next door to tell my administrator, Ginny, and Web programmer, Ryan. Jerry Fields, who'd been hanging around our office ever since I'd put Beverly on leave, was chatting with Ryan about the alert Fred had distributed to the third-floor folks.

We gathered together at Beverly's old desk.

"Dear Colleagues," I read, my voice steady.

> I want to alert you that the joint University/federal investigation of fraud and other improper governmental activities . . . is likely to come to public notice . . . We're advised by the US attorney leading this investigation that the search warrant . . . will become accessible by the public today or tomorrow . . . direct any media inquires . . . to me . . . I will explain:
> The University is cooperating with a federal investigation into allegations of fraudulent activities by a former employee . . . allegations were reported as whistleblower complaint with the university. The employee was served with

a search warrant on Monday, October 30 . . .
subsequently resigned . . .

We were all abuzz with the news. Jerry, wide-eyed and beaming, was rich with Fred stories.

"Dr. Stone forwarded the alert to everyone. He wasn't happy
at all. He was staggering around the mail room groaning," Jerry
chirped.

"What did Dr. Stone say?" I asked.

"Ah . . . I don't think he said anything in particular," he stammered, befuddled. Ginny rolled her eyes. Not a big fan of Jerry's,
she described him as a "lost puppy dog."

At six o'clock I suggested we call it a night. I went back to my
office to send some emails before hitting the road.

The telephone rang at home on Sunday, November 5. I was
working with my now teenage daughter, Judith, on her UC college application, due at the end of the month. I couldn't believe
she was already a senior and ready to leave the nest.

"Hello," I said as I picked up the telephone.

"Fred, here, I need to talk to you." He sounded worried. I was
surprised both by his call and the fact that he still had my number.

"Oh, Fred, hello," I said tentatively. "How are you?"

He didn't reply with the niceties one usually expects on a Sunday.

"The vice president for agriculture was briefed," he began.

I listened intently. The vice president for agriculture, Anthony
Roberts, was responsible for the agricultural arm of the university and its statewide infrastructure of county programs, agricultural organizations and businesses, commodity groups, and
you name it. I'd worked in this branch in the president's office
in Oakland and reported directly to VP Gloria Jones in the
eighties. Roberts, the new VP, was a highly regarded and effective leader of the university's massive agricultural sector.

"Was this an official brief?" I asked, attempting to figure out
what he was trying to tell me.

"Is this related to Beverly?" I asked.

After some hemming and hawing, Fred finally came to the point. "I just thought you'd want to know; after all, this will affect you."

"Affect me? What do you mean? How would this affect me?" I asked.

"You should just think about it. I thought you'd want to know." Fred said good-bye and quickly hung up.

I didn't want to know and tried not to think about it. Judith had finished her college essay, and I was proud of her accomplishments. We'd visited a number of schools, but she was the most gung-ho about UC, either at Los Angeles or Davis.

A friend of Judith's, Jake Greenberg, was coming over for dinner. They had been friends for years after meeting at a Bat Mitzvah party. Jake attended high school with Judith and was captain of the rugby team that traveled all over the United States winning tournaments.

I'd asked Judith what Jake liked to eat. Her answer was steak. She insisted that he'd eat that and nothing else. I bought a couple of New York steaks, and baked some potatoes. I also made a salad with lots of veggies, apples, and nuts.

"Hi Jake," I said when I answered the door. He was very tall and towered over me.

"What's up?" he grinned, as he shook my hand firmly. His manners were impeccable.

"Come in," I said warmly.

Judith was hovering near by and escorted him away quickly. They danced to her room, and I returned to the kitchen. The sound of very loud music filled the house. Now seventeen, she was beautiful, smart, and sweet.

I set the table and served dinner, then knocked on her door. The music was blaring and the house was pulsating. So I called her cell phone and she picked up.

"We'll be right there, Mom," she said sweetly.

She was correct about what Jake would eat. I gave him the bigger steak and cut the other one in half after removing all the fat. We weren't exactly strict vegetarians since we also enjoyed a good steak now and then. Jake politely declined both potatoes and salad, although he consumed three large glasses of low-fat milk.

"So, Jake, I hear you're the captain of the rugby team," I said, trying not to embarrass Judith, who probably would have preferred if we ate in silence.

Jake said it was a good year. Worried that I might be focusing too much unwanted attention on him, I changed the subject.

"All these college applications are bringing back fond memories of all the fun I had at Berkeley," I said, trying to make conversation. Judith and I had discussed her applying to my alma mater—but we both thought going away to college meant leaving the Bay Area.

"My mom went to Berkeley," Jake added as he picked up his glass of milk.

"What does she do now?" I asked, genuinely interested in a fellow Berkeley grad.

"My mom's a criminologist," he answered, glancing at our dog Figgy, who'd been parked under the table, patiently waiting for any food that might drop.

Imagine that, I thought to myself while resisting the urge to tell them both right then and there about my whistleblower experience. Figgy's tail wagged as he emerged, hoping for some meat. Sadly, I pointed him back to his dog food in the kitchen.

"I hear you work at Davis," Jake said.

"Yes, I'm in the Food, Health and Society Department," I nodded, reflecting silently about my secret life at work.

Suddenly, dinner was over, and they were leaving to visit a friend. I heard them laughing as they got into Jake's car and drove off. While I did the dishes, I mused at the thought that my daughter would soon be off to college, hopefully at the University of California.

I had completely forgotten about Fred's weird telephone call.

The next day was Monday, November 6, and I left for work

very early. I needed to review all the questionable pieces of the budget amendment. Beverly's original budget was confusing and convoluted. She'd left a spreadsheet on her desk, and although the math was perfect, I was suspicious that her supply budget was out of whack and highly exaggerated, but I hadn't yet unteased it. Beverly's administrative assistant, Rebecca Fukumoto, was researching the pieces for me.

Rebecca, or Becky as she was now called, a single mom raising two active teen boys, had been Beverly's personal assistant for a couple of years and telecommuted three days a week from home. I'd met her once years ago at a party and was impressed by her calm demeanor. Because Rebecca worked closely with Beverly, I believed she held the answer to many of my questions. However, I wasn't clear about her relationship with Beverly, and I couldn't risk talking to her about my concerns.

While I was drafting my response to the USDA's questions, my telephone rang.

"Hello, this is Amy Block Joy."

"It's Becky. Something's weird with that spreadsheet," she said, sounding uncharacteristically frantic.

"What?"

"Got a pen handy? I've got all sorts of screwy items that seem to be placed in an account named, here let me spell it for you: R-S-E-Q-U-I-N-O-X. Does that ring a bell?"

"I think RS stands for Raymond Savage." I'd remembered the EQUINOX file where I'd found the DVD camcorder purchase order.

"Yep. That must be it." Becky agreed. "Well, it looks like Bev created a special account for Dr. Savage!"

Egad, Beverly's been providing funds to Raymond without my knowledge. Does Rebecca know that this could be misappropriation?

"How much is in the account?"

"So far, about eighty thousand dollars in salaries and benefits. But I'm not done."

Rebecca rattled off the information from this account that I'd never seen before. I was having trouble keeping up, but I didn't want to give Rebecca a clue that this account was unknown to me. Suddenly, in the middle of all this, my office door burst open. Fred waltzed in, looking like he'd seen a ghost. He started talking to me; he didn't seem to notice that I was on the telephone.

"It's bad, it's really bad . . ." Fred said shaking his head.

I told Rebecca I'd call her back and hung up.

Fred looked drained and exhausted. "I'm supposed to meet with Franklin," Fred began, as he picked up the stuff I'd put on a chair next to my printer. He dropped all my amendment spreadsheets and drafts on the floor as he plopped down, moaning.

"Oh," was all I could say. Franklin was the assistant executive vice-chancellor.

"Frank's a decent guy, but if he's got questions, you might be better off jumping out his window," Fred continued in a dark voice.

"Fred, what happened?" I asked again.

"Franklin's going to grill me about your whistleblower report."

Fred was holding his face in his hands and then suddenly sat up.

"I've spoken to Raymond for an hour!" he said angrily. "You knew about her travel! You approved it!" His voice became accusatory.

"I did not," I said, annoyed. "We've been over this Fred," I continued calmly. "You know that no one consulted with me about her travel."

We sat there in silence.

"As you already know, Raymond's computer was taken by the auditors!"

Fred looked up and watched my reaction.

"What?" I said, shocked. "No, I didn't know. When did this happen?"

He got up from the chair and left in a hurry. *Fred thinks I'm responsible for Raymond's computer seizure. Could he have found out that I met with the police and the feds?*

After Fred left my office, Ginny knocked on the door. She had heard Fred's voice in my office.

"He made a special trip to my office to bring me the news that Dr. Savage's computer was taken by the auditors."

Ginny nodded. "I'd already heard about that through the grapevine," she added.

Before calling Rebecca back to finish our conversation, I thought I'd inquire about Rebecca's relationship with Beverly. It was awkward for me not to know. If Beverly was still communicating with Rebecca, she'd likely deny it. So I asked Ginny.

"Ginny, I just got off the phone with Rebecca. Do you think Beverly might be hounding her?"

"Nope, no way," said Ginny concretely, then added, "They parted ways when Beverly hit her up for some cash."

"Beverly borrowed money from Rebecca? Do you recall when?" I asked.

"Rebecca loaned Beverly several hundred dollars when Beverly needed cash for a mortgage payment. Sometime last spring," Ginny said.

"Why Rebecca?" I asked Ginny.

"She tried everybody! She managed to get Becky to hand some over by promising her a higher salary. Beverly even wrote up a reclassification. I doubt that paperwork went anywhere," Ginny told me. My mouth fell open. Ginny was correct, I'd not seen any request to reclassify Rebecca.

"What kind of job did she promise?"

"A budget analyst position," Ginny said. "You know that Becky's been actually doing the number crunching for Beverly all these years," Ginny sighed.

I wondered if this was the money that Beverly found to pay back the university for the camcorder. Poor Rebecca!

Armed with more information, I called Rebecca back and asked her to label each questionable item on the spreadsheet and fax it to me. Neither of us talked about the investigation, and I never asked her about the loan. I promised myself I wasn't going to get emotionally entangled in any more of Beverly's carnage.

When I received her two-page fax, I saw that the first page was the spreadsheet with Rebecca's notations. The second page was a copy of an account created by Beverly for Raymond. Beverly named it EQUINOX, and the spreadsheet contained two vague entries. The first was $150,000 for "Nutrition Education Training" and the second, $127,075, was for "Nutrition Education for Adult and Youth." I rushed the spreadsheet and the account number for Raymond over to the auditor's office.

Raymond, the world-renowned scientist, wasn't doing nutrition education training for poor families. It looked to me like Beverly was funneling off huge amounts of money to him, and he was spending it!

Wednesday, November 8, turned out to be another Fred day. Late in the afternoon he called me to come up to his office. He said he was meeting with Dean Gabriel Fitzpatrick in an hour, and he needed to talk to me right away. He started zinging questions at me before I'd even shut his door.

"How do you explain all this missing money?" was his first, followed by, "and the conference room equipment also needs an explanation."

Astonished, I sat down in the chair and listened. Fred was marveling that all this money appeared to be missing. *But I believed he knew where the money was—and who was spending it. Was this why Beverly was so popular?*

"Fred, is this what you discussed with the vice-chancellor?" I asked.

Fred glared at me and wouldn't answer; instead he changed the subject.

"Darci's being questioned."

"What?" I asked. "Why is Darci being questioned?" Now I was utterly confused. *Did Beverly provide money to her, too?*

"Kickbacks." The word bounced around his office.

"Kickbacks?" I asked startled. "Was Beverly giving Darci kickbacks? What kind? For what?" Now Fred had my full attention, but he still wasn't making any sense.

"Raymond is so gullible! Why'd he get involved with Beverly?" Fred whimpered. "They're looking into misappropriation . . . some of it was for the equipment in the conference room." I watched him agonize over the meeting he was going to have with Dean Fitzpatrick, who'd want concrete answers to these questions. When I tried to ask him again about kickbacks, he groaned.

I waited for him to calm down. I doubted he wanted my support, but I wasn't sure why I was sitting there. Did he think I knew something useful? The auditors told me nothing; he knew more than I did. Besides, I wasn't planning on sharing my thoughts on Raymond. He finally lifted his head and looked at me sadly.

"Fred, I don't know what to say," was all I could think of as our eyes met. I felt sorry for him; obviously he was suffering.

I was about to ask Fred about the equipment in the conference room but decided to wait. Something was bothering him, and I wanted to find out what it was.

We sat there in silence until he seemed to find his voice. "I'm not taking the sword for Beverly," he concluded, becoming very red in the face.

I thought he was done, so I got up to leave.

"Sit down," he said. "It's your turn now. Do you know what that means?" Fred asked pointedly.

"Spell it out, Fred?" I shot back.

"What it means," he said vaguely, "what it now means for *you*?" he added.

"For me?" I repeated. "I'm not following."

"This is all going to affect you," he said aggressively.

I waited for him to finish.

"It will personally affect you and your future. Think about it."

"What specifically do you mean? Don't be vague," I asked, trying to get him to cough it up.

"Think hard," he stammered. "Think of the worst-case scenario for you!" I stood up and boldly headed to the door. He continued to follow me with his eyes. Obviously, feeling sorry for Fred was a mistake. He was out for blood.

Fred's behavior felt like harassment. His veiled threats were unpleasant. He wanted to make me nervous, probably thinking under pressure I'd crack. I decided I should report all these conversations to Vice-Chancellor Taylor-Starr, the LDO. I was supposed to be protected from retaliation.

I sent an email to the LDO and requested a meeting. I said that I was receiving veiled threats and I wanted some guidance. Our meeting was set for Monday, November 13.

The following day passed without much ado, although Fred saw me in the mail room chatting with Ginny and asked me to step into his office. He shut the door behind us.

"I saw Dean Fitzpatrick," he began, "and he asked me to cool it."

I was pleased. Someone's giving Fred good advice.

But Fred wasn't interested in cooling it.

"Do you know what 'it' is?" he asked.

I knew exactly what Dean Fitzpatrick was saying and so did Fred.

"What do you think it means?" I said, trying to stifle a giggle.

"How would I know?" he snorted.

I sat in his chair waiting for the thunderbolt to strike him. But nothing happened. I mumbled something about having to get back to work and left in a hurry, leaving Fred slumped in his chair pondering "it."

On Friday, November 10, three auditors arrived to remove the files from our offices. They allowed me to watch as they boxed up all the files and removed them. After clearing the stuff from the top of Beverly's desk, Director Grant of audit services removed the duct tape from Beverly's drawers and took out all the files. I had personally sealed her drawers with the tape on August 28.

I asked Director Grant if I could review Beverly's desk drawer files before they carted them away. I said I had a legitimate business need to see and copy any information from her desk so I could do my job.

Director Grant agreed, asking one of the auditors to over-

see my review. Joseph Parker, an older, serious man with a distinguished salt-and-pepper beard, stood next to me. Director
Grant moved to the file room to supervise the work of the other
auditors. I watched him walk over to the file cabinet where I
had discovered the fraudulent DVD camcorder purchase order
in March.

Joseph opened the drawer and handed me a bunch of files.
One caught my eye immediately. Labeled "Beverly Benford,"
the file contained emails for at least three computer purchases.
These purchases might have been completely appropriate,
except for copies of correspondence showing that Beverly had
sold them.

There was email from Beverly to someone who bought one or
two computers from Beverly's Internet ad. Another email was
from Beverly to her daughter confirming she'd shipped her a
computer and wanted a check in return. Beverly even used the
university's FedEx account to send it to her daughter and had
the receipt in the file. When I saw her selling price I wanted to
scream. Beverly overcharged her own flesh and blood!

I handed the file back to Joseph.

"You'll want to keep this one handy," I whispered to him.

"Thanks," was all he said after he glanced poker-faced at the
email. I had the feeling that this wasn't news to the auditors.
They'd probably already reviewed her emails.

Joseph opened Beverly's top desk drawer. Obviously a junk
drawer because everything was stuffed and in disarray, he pulled
out papers and handed me things that weren't relevant to the
investigation. In the stack of miscellaneous paper, I unfolded
some heart-shaped notes and pulled out a card.

The heart notes were from Darci! I read the notes out loud to
Ginny and noted the cute little "kisses" on them.

"Love, love, love xxxxx—D."

I called Ginny over to see Darci's kisses. "Look what Beverly
had in her drawer!" She told me that Beverly was always going
up to see Darci.

"Why would she keep these?" I wondered out loud.

Joseph, who was still working nearby, offered a viable explanation. "They must have meant something to her."

"Oh, yeah, she loved Darci!" Ginny explained. "She had petite Darci twisted around her little finger."

"Why?" I asked mortified.

"Because Beverly didn't want you to have any friends!"

As I took in what Ginny had suggested, I handed Ryan the card. On the envelope was one word, "Ryan" in my handwriting.

"Special delivery! From Beverly's desk to you," I said looking again at the writing on the envelope as he began to tear it open.

"Ryan!" I exclaimed, suddenly recognizing it. "Is this from your baby's shower? What's it doing in Beverly's desk?"

The auditors seemed to be eager to go. All the files were packed and everything on and in Beverly's desk was gone. Loads of boxes were put on carts and taken out to the parking lot. I wanted to jokingly say good luck but thought it wouldn't be appropriate, so I waved good-bye.

After they left, we gathered around Ryan as he pulled out the card. The card was signed by all of us in 2004 but was missing the gift card we had paid for with our contributions. He told us that Beverly said she'd left the card at home and kept promising to bring it to work and give to him. Ginny and I reconstructed that Beverly collected money from the group for a $250 Target Gift Card for their new baby. She never gave it to Ryan.

"She kept telling me she'd left the card at home," Ryan told us. "I eventually stopped asking." He was visibly angry, even outraged.

"Beverly stole from your baby!" Ginny announced with disgust.

"How low can one get?" I said, feeling sad for Ryan. "I'm really sorry, Ryan," I said as he shook his head in disbelief.

Beverly didn't discriminate—she screwed everyone.

On Monday, November 13, I met with the executive vice-chancellor and LDO, Franklin Taylor-Starr, in his office. A tall, suit-and-tie dignified man, he had an honest and genuine sincerity about him. I immediately felt that this was a person I could completely trust.

"I'm honored to finally meet you," I said as I shook his hand.

"Yes, it's good to meet you, too," he said. "Please have a seat."

We sat at a round table in his office. I'd prepared a report of all my conversations with Fred, including the gossip, titled, "Interactions with Dr. Fred Stone." I handed it to him.

We didn't discuss my blow-by-blow details of every conversation I'd had with Fred. Instead, he asked me general questions about my work and the nutrition program I directed. I summarized my whistleblower report that had found its way to him.

Executive Vice-Chancellor Taylor-Starr provided a detailed explanation of the policy that protected a whistleblower from retaliation. I listened and took notes.

I apologized to him for sending so many emails but said that I wanted to be sure that I was documenting all the events.

"I support your efforts to comply with university policy," he told me.

At the end of the meeting he said, "People I work with usually call me Frank or Franklin."

"Thanks for meeting with me, uh, Frank," I said as I left his office. I'd never met an executive vice-chancellor before, and I was in awe of him. I was confident that the investigation was in very good hands.

On November 21, 2006, I went upstairs to get my mail. In the stack was the official letter and six-page investigative report clearing me of all charges.

I also received a copy of the investigative report, which included the field work on each allegation. The final statement on page 6 reported, "The purpose of our investigation was to determine the validity . . . The investigation was performed in September 2006. The allegations were not substantiated...and the case is closed."

Although I was officially cleared, this investigation wouldn't see the light of day, and I was told to keep it under wraps.

Fred had already approved my budget, so my next task was to prepare the final report of last year's accomplishments. This was a big job, and in the past Beverly was a major contributor to preparing tables of nutrition and health data collected from 120,000 children and adults. I hadn't been allowed to replace her position so I was pretty much stuck doing the work myself.

Just before Thanksgiving, I found more evidence! Someone had anonymously put a five-page list of our program equipment in my mailbox. The list contained descriptions, dates, and costs of numerous computers, laptops, printers, and other program equipment purchased from 1998 to 2006.

I could easily locate equipment that I'd approved. However, tons of other stuff I'd never seen before popped out!

Scanning the report, several big pricey items surprised me, including two departmental servers and accessories, expensive teleconferencing equipment for the department's conference room, and equipment for Raymond's office renovation. None of these items were legit, and I certainly hadn't approved them.

I recalled Fred's admission of missing money, and his worry about the conference room equipment. *Yikes! Is this what Fred meant by kickbacks? No wonder Fred was so nervous about answering question!*

I copied the report and drove over to the auditor's office as fast as I could. When I arrived they seemed to already know about these purchases. We went into their meeting room. Juliet and Lawrence asked me specific questions about the servers and the conference equipment.

"Did your program require the use of two servers?"

"Well, the way we calculate the use of any shared equipment is by prorating usage. I very much doubt that our program required more than 10 percent of one server. The USDA would approve only the prorated cost. We shouldn't have been charged for two servers and their accessories."

"Did you use the conferencing equipment in the Foster Room?"

"Absolutely not. Any cost to our program for this equipment would be totally inappropriate. This was used by the department folks and many other departments all over campus." I was irate.

"What about the third-floor office renovations?"

"The USDA wouldn't have approved third-floor office renovations because in the audit in 2003 they put in their report that renovations for the department weren't allowable. They would only approve renovations for the space we occupied on the first floor."

I was calculating the cost of these items and came up with about $100,000. Rebecca found $80,000 in salaries and benefits. Beverly's spreadsheet identified another $277,000, totaling $457,000. Was there more?

"I wonder if this is related to Beverly's spreadsheet?" I asked, hoping that they'd give me a clue.

They told me that they were still working on it, and they couldn't really tell me, which was their standard answer to all my questions.

The only viable information source I had was Fred, who, though better than nothing, probably wasn't the most reliable.

I also did a lot of speculating and tried to deduce information by the questions that the auditors asked. Before we were done, Juliet asked one and it was a doozy!

"Did Beverly ever send emails for you?" Juliet asked.

"Yes. I'd send her information, and she'd forward it using a list-serve of the statewide folks in the program."

"Did she ever send emails from your computer?"

"Use my computer?" I thought about that for a few minutes.

"No, she didn't send emails for me from my computer. I didn't give her permission to use my computer." I was horrified at the thought of Beverly using my computer.

"Do you think she ever used it? Do you recall anything out of the ordinary on your computer?" Juliet asked.

I sat there thinking. *Are they telling me that Beverly used my computer?*

"I only recall one incident when I had to call tech support

because the settings of my computer had suddenly changed. We had just moved downstairs from the third floor," I said, "so it had to have been around October 2001."

The auditors told me that they believed Beverly had found my password around that time.

"How were the settings changed?" Juliet asked.

"All my emails were stored chronologically. I never changed the settings. However, one day I turned on my computer and discovered that my email directory had been rearranged alphabetically. Do you think Beverly was looking for something?" I asked. Neither Juliet nor Lawrence answered, though they asked me to review my emails to see if I could find any specific evidence that Beverly might have written or sent emails from my computer.

I wondered if I would have noticed if someone used my computer. I received a lot of emails from more than three hundred people, so it was going to be a slow process to review everything. I had a long-standing practice of never deleting emails.

The auditors requested a copy of my hard drive. I provided my written permission to send my computer to a firm in Emeryville to make an imprint of the hard drive. The imprint is a photographic copy that cannot be altered. Joseph came with me to my office to remove my computer. A tech person from the dean's office met us there to copy my hard drive onto a replacement computer.

It turned out to be easy to find evidence that Beverly was using my computer. She'd sent many of my emails to herself by forwarding them from my sent box to her inbox. I continued to look to see if she'd sent any emails, but I had over a hundred thousand emails so it wasn't going to be easy. No wonder she seemed so in tune with me. She was reading my emails!

I asked Ginny and Ryan if Beverly ever used my office when I wasn't there.

"All the time, are you kidding?" Ginny replied and Ryan nodded.

"She was really cozy in there, especially when you went on sabbatical." This was my four-month study leave at the end of 2005.

"Do you know why?" I asked.

"Well, most of the time it was to use your telephone. She said that your office was private and she had to make confidential calls about the budget," Ginny recalled. "Last year she was really worried about Tessa," Ginny added. "Then there was that staff meeting. Remember?" she asked, looking at Ryan.

"Oh, yeah." Ryan looked embarrassed. "Beverly had a tirade. She called Tessa a traitor, said 'she's going to be sorry she messed with me,'" he said, looking pale. "Beverly was in a rage."

"What happened between Beverly and Tessa?" I asked. "Beverly said they had a spat and Tessa resigned," I added.

"Well, it wasn't a spat. Tessa found out about a trip Beverly took to Florida," Ginny announced. "Tessa believed this wasn't business and tried to alert the department chair. She waited until Beverly left on her to trip to Washington DC."

Ryan and Ginny shared the whole Tessa saga, while I stood there silently listening. Finally, I was now going to hear what happened to Tessa!

Beverly had hired Tessa because she was a trained bookkeeper. Tessa had been working in the office for a few years. After Beverly left for the DC conference, Tessa came to work all aglitter.

"I remember that day because Tessa came to work all dressed up."

"Remember, Ryan?" Ginny asked. "We teased her, asking if she had a job interview or something big. She was wearing make-up and a skirt! She told us that she was meeting with Dr. Savage and showed us the travel documents that she'd printed."

"Tessa told us that she'd researched Beverly's trip to Florida. Beverly claimed travel for a nutrition conference. Tessa looked up all nutrition meetings and conferences in and around Florida on that week of Beverly's trip. There just weren't any nutrition meetings."

"Beverly went to Florida!" I was floored. None of Beverly's travel fraud that I'd seen was out-of-state; this was clearly over the top as Beverly herself knew our funds were for in-state only travel, with the exception of our national DC conference.

"Yep. Beverly's daughter was graduating from nursing school in Florida and voila!" Ginny said. "No surprise that she wanted the university to fund her trip and vacation to Florida.

"Tessa was furious and found the courage to tell Dr. Savage," Ginny exclaimed.

"What happened when Tessa told him?" I asked, recalling that Raymond never mentioned Tessa's allegation of travel fraud.

"Tessa went up to see Dr. Savage feeling confident and returned quite agitated. Dr. Savage told her the research on the Florida trip didn't prove a thing. So what if she couldn't find a meeting on the Internet. She told him that she'd have to resign, and he tried to convince her to stay. He even offered her another job! He promised not to tell Beverly. But she was too freaked out to stay."

I was holding back my anger. *Raymond told me a number of things that turned out not to be true.*

"Did you know that Beverly was supposed to go to a national meeting in DC and never showed up?" I asked. "I heard that Dr. Savage made Beverly return to Davis because Tessa resigned."

"Who told you that?" Ginny asked.

"Dr. Savage told me a bunch of baloney, saying the office was a mess and poor Beverly was stressed," I scoffed, recalling that Raymond actually blamed me for stressing Beverly.

"Well, he was correct about one thing—Beverly was a mess!" Ginny said.

"She was furious when Dr. Savage made her return," Ginny continued. "Beverly called Tessa a traitor and a freakin' nut. She told us that Tessa told Dr. Savage disgusting lies about her and tried to get her fired. Boy, was she spewing venom.

"Tessa resigned because she was fearful of Beverly's response. We all wondered who would be next," Ginny explained. "After that incident, we figured nothing was going to happen. We believed Dr. Savage, the department chair, was protecting Beverly," Ginny added. "We were all terrified of Beverly, and for that matter, of Dr. Savage."

Ryan was nodding and looking worried.

"Ginny, you may recall that I tried asking you and Ryan about Tessa but both of you told me to ask Beverly," I reminded them.

"We were too afraid to tell you," Ginny said sadly. "I'm sorry that I didn't trust you, but Beverly had all of us believing you were on her side."

Ryan nodded in agreement. "Ginny, would you be willing to tell the auditors what happened in September 2005?" Ginny nodded eagerly.

"And how about you, Ryan?"

He nodded, although I noted that he wasn't as eager as Ginny.

I called Juliet and gave her a heads-up about Ginny and Ryan's information. I heard later that Ginny, Ryan, and Rebecca were all going to be interviewed. I could hardly wait.

On Wednesday, November 30, 2006, the third floor departmental folks received a surprise visit from the auditors.

It turns out that our program money had been used to purchase very expensive equipment for Raymond's department. Some of my colleagues had computers and fancy printers, some legit, some questionable, that I didn't know about. In addition, expensive teleconferencing equipment and the two servers were located in offices that weren't part of our program. *Was this the money that was diverted most likely by Beverly for Raymond's "general departmental" use?*

December 2006 seemed to go by very quickly. I finished our 125-page final report on December 9, and sent it to the USDA for review, pleased with the program's positive results.

The auditors called me to come over to review a document. I met with them in their reception area and confirmed that the document was indeed familiar and the signature was mine. As I turned to go back to my office, I recalled something and froze on the spot.

"There's something I need to tell you that I just remembered." I turned around to face them. Juliet and Lawrence were still standing in the reception area. I walked back and leaned against their file cabinet.

I started speaking rapidly. I had to tell them no matter what the consequences.

"A number of years ago, way before any of this, I signed some blank forms." The memory came back in a flash.

"This was considered standard practice in my department prior to a vacation," I added.

They were quiet, probably stunned.

"It happened when I was leaving for a New York vacation. Beverly followed me to my car and said that she needed some paperwork signed right there on the spot. She was holding forms and a pen for me to sign. The forms weren't filled in. I felt pressured. I knew that other faculty did it, and I caved."

We all remained standing.

"When I told Beverly I was uncomfortable and I thought she should wait, she gave me a song and dance about me not trusting her. She reminded me that my vacation shouldn't cause the program to grind to a halt. She went on and on about a printer that was already ordered by telephone.

"I was weak." I could picture Beverly in the parking lot talking to me and my need to get going.

"I pre-signed a few forms in the parking lot," I repeated. "This happened in 2000."

Both Juliet and Lawrence were silent. I continued.

"When I returned from my trip, I told Beverly I wasn't pre-signing anything no matter what other people did in the department. I recall that Beverly didn't argue. Beverly did show me the new printer and the other items purchased as if to say—'See, you can trust me!'

"I'm telling you this because I thought you needed to know and I'm sorry it happened."

A couple of weeks later, Juliet called me to let me know they found nothing improper had resulted from this. Even though this reflected poorly on me, I was relieved that I'd told them. I had been way too trusting.

In January 2007 our program was to be administrated under the dean's office instead of the Food, Health and Society Department. Ginny asked me if this was good.

"Absolutely," I said. "The dean's office will treat us fairly." We could now function under the administrative control of people who wanted the program to succeed and be operationally correct.

No longer held captive by Fred, I was pleased that my new supervisor was Associate Dean Percival Grossman. I immediately requested a reclassification for Rebecca and Ginny. Both of them had assumed some of Beverly's higher level responsibilities. I also requested that the two positions left vacant by Beverly and Tessa be refilled.

Now that things were moving in the right direction, I was ready to build up the program. Finally, I began to relax.

During the month of January 2007 the auditors finished their interviews with my staff. Both Rebecca and Ginny seemed pleased to have an opportunity to talk about Beverly. Ryan, who was usually cheerful anyway, was actually beaming.

Although I wasn't supposed to ask them about their interviews, it was Ryan who burst forth with a tidbit.

"I told Lawrence all about my shopping trips with Beverly," Ryan began.

"Really," I said.

"Yeah," Ryan stated, "she'd call me at home and offer to take me to work, then on our way back home, she'd stop at Fry's."

"You went with Beverly to Fry's!?" I exclaimed, practically shouting.

"Well, yes," Ryan said with a big grin, "she needed a strong guy to carry the stuff into her house." Ryan was a tall, muscular guy, and he held up his arms to prove it!

"OK," I said to Ryan, "tell us what she bought!"

"TVs, stereos, the big items," he said. "She told me that she was paying by credit card, even waving it around for me to see. But one time, when she was talking to the guy at Fry's, I heard her mention an account number that didn't sound like a credit card." His voice lowered as we gathered closer.

"I asked her in the car if there was a problem with her credit card," he continued. "I was feeling funny about being there. She told me that the TV was for the program. She said someone at the conference was picking it up."

Ginny piped in. "Yes! I remember her bringing that stupid TV set to the conference! It was strange. Every room already had a TV set."

"Did you bring the TV into her hotel room?" I asked Ryan.

Both Ginny and Ryan looked at each other.

"Yes, she made me carry it into her room. And it sat there until we left."

"No wonder Beverly never invited me into her hotel room!" I said. "Ryan, what happened? Did she sell it?"

"Nope. She got the hotel to put it back into the van and when we got back to Sacramento she made me carry it back into her house."

Ryan looked serious. "She stopped asking me to go to Fry's after that."

Our next conference was scheduled for February 5 and 6, 2007, at our usual location, the Clarion Hotel in San Francisco. I was preparing my presentation on the new administrative procedures. I wasn't planning on mentioning that the procedures were developed to prevent future criminal activity. Instead, Percy planned to talk about the investigation. He expected that people might be worried, and his job was to reduce anxiety.

I met with Percy in late January about the conference and my request to hire new staff. He said everything was on hold until the investigation was completed. He estimated it would be another month or so. Although this made sense from an institutional standpoint, I was disappointed and worried that my small group, especially Rebecca, might run out of steam.

He did agree to provide short-term stipends to Ginny and Rebecca, who were both getting lower pay than other employees doing the same job. I was relieved to be able to tell them that their hard work and dedication would be compensated.

On Sunday, February 4, I drove down to the Clarion Hotel for our two-day statewide conference. I was excited to see and talk to people again now with the investigation winding down. This would be our first conference without Beverly. I checked in to my room and picked up the telephone to call the front desk. I wanted to speak to Brenda, our hotel contact, but I had a slip of the tongue and asked for Benford, Beverly's last name.

"I'm Amy Joy with UC. I'd like to speak with Benford."

The receptionist responded, "Ms. Benford hasn't checked in yet."

I swallowed hard. "This must be a mistake," I said to the woman on the telephone, "I'm Amy Joy and I'm actually looking for Brenda."

"Oh, Brenda. She's not working this evening. She'll be here tomorrow at seven in the morning."

"Has Ginny Buckner checked in?" I asked in a bit of a panic.

"I'll connect you with the hotel operator."

I waited, trying to figure out what happened.

"Hello," Ginny answered the telephone.

"Ginny, I'm not sure how to tell you this . . ."

"Amy, are you all right?" Ginny asked, hearing my agitation.

I couldn't even speak. I went to Ginny's room. When I explained what had happened, she called the hotel operator and asked for Beverly Benford. Sure enough the operator also reported that Beverly hadn't checked in yet. After some probing questions, Ginny found out that Beverly had the conference suite reserved!

"She's got that room again!" Ginny grumbled.

"What?" I was flabbergasted.

"Yes," Ginny said. "Since you never took it, Beverly always

claimed it for herself. She made Ryan and I swear we'd never tell you."

"How did she keep it off the master bill?" I asked curious.

"Oh, the bill you saw wasn't the final invoice," Ginny told me. Ginny sat down on the bed looking worried.

"I'm sorry I couldn't talk to you or trust you," Ginny admitted. "Beverly threatened me, saying that I'd be fired. She said you thought I was making mistakes right and left; she said you called me inept and stupid."

Ginny sounded determined, even tough, as she came to grips with the past. Tears came to my eyes as I heard the details of Beverly's rage and hostility. Ginny also alluded to a more personal threat. Beverly threatened Ginny that she'd reveal personal information to make me and others believe that Ginny was emotionally unstable. I longed to comfort Ginny, but now wasn't the time to try to make amends for Beverly's long-time abuse.

"Let's make a date to talk when we're back in Davis," I added softly.

I stood up and began to regain my determination. "We have a job to do," I announced. "Do you have any idea how Beverly get on our list? She's not even a university employee."

"Beverly probably called the hotel and sweet-talked Brenda," Ginny suggested.

"We should've warned Brenda about Beverly and the fraud," I said, realizing that Brenda was also a victim.

Ryan arrived, and we updated him on the situation. He went down to inquire at the front desk and confirmed that Beverly was on the list.

I left a telephone message for Percy at his home and sent a "Help!" email to Frank. It was Sunday evening, and I figured I'd have to wait until Monday morning for help to arrive.

However, that evening Frank and Percy notified the hotel, and I met with hotel security, who confirmed that Beverly's name had been on the list. The hotel promptly removed her name and promised that our conference wouldn't be disrupted.

We never saw her, although plenty of her friends were attending the event, including Darci, who avoided me like the plague.

The conference went without a hitch. People appeared friendly enough, relaxed and upbeat. I felt good after my presentation of the new administrative procedures. Percy's forward-looking speech was well received. Although several of my dinner invitations were declined by former chums, I didn't think much about it. I was happy and optimistic about the future.

On February 21, 2007, Carrie Peyton Dahlberg, a *Sacramento Bee* reporter, requested an interview. She had recently done a story on Raymond's work with EQUINOX. She left a message for me at work that she was doing a follow-up story and that someone suggested that she talk to me.

I called Frank and told him that I didn't feel comfortable speaking to a reporter. Frank advised me that as director I should agree to be interviewed and that the university's legal team would guide me on what to say and what not to say.

I was instructed to talk about the benefits of the program and to refer questions about the investigation to the university vice-chancellor for communications. I called Carrie back and she interviewed me over the telephone.

Carrie was intelligent, polite, and a good interviewer. She was also cunning and tried every which way to ask about Raymond, but I declined, as instructed, and referred her to the vice-chancellor of communications. After the interview she read me back her notes. I prepared a report of our forty-minute interview to make it clear that I'd followed university procedures.

> Discussion with Reporter—Yes, someone spoke to her!
> I just got off the telephone with Carrie . . .
> During the discussion, which was primarily about the work we do to improve health . . .
> she started asking . . . about the funds . . . initially reasonable questions until she popped,
> "Are you using Equinox funds?" in the middle

of a teaching people to cook dialogue! . . . then
it was again about Equinox . . . do you have
money problems . . . any employee problems
. . . I asked if someone from the university
talked to her . . . she told me she had done a
story on Equinox . . . so I asked if someone
suggested she talk to me . . . she didn't really
answer . . . said she received a telephone call
but could not reveal the source . . .

The next day, February 22, I received another interesting
telephone call. My colleague and friend, Angela Sharply, from
Southern California called with a warning. A negative letter
was circulating about me.

"You need to get a copy of the letter right away," Angela
advised me.

"Who has the letter?" I asked.

"Go to the highest person at Davis," Angela said. Politically
astute and diplomatic, I trusted her.

"Ireta wrote the letter and you need to see it," Angela
warned me.

"Ireta Koskernof?" I said, surprised. Ireta was a talented colleague stuck in Mendocino, California, who liked to stir up
trouble. I'd worked with her for years, even asking her to serve
on committees. But most of my attempts to be friendly had
been rejected.

"The one and only," said Angela. Ireta had a reputation for
being smart and sassy and, more recently, unhappy probably
due to not getting a higher level position at the university.

"She wanted me to meet with her to follow up on some issues
from our conference two weeks ago. She seemed friendly," I
remarked, feeling foolish.

"Well," Angela began, "you may feel differently after you read
what she's written.

"And, just so you know, the anonymous person at the end of
the letter is Patricia," she added. "You need to know who's not

in your camp. I know you wrote a very positive letter for her promotion, but . . ." I wrote down her observations and tried not to panic.

"Please leave me out of this for now—I have to get along with these people!" Angela continued, sounding fearful. "I hate to say this, but my colleagues can get nasty, and who knows what might happen if people find out that I told you." I agreed not to use her name when I made my inquiry about the letter.

"What kind of letter is it?" I asked.

"It's a petition to remove you from office!" Angela was very articulate and didn't mince words. "Ireta said that she was retiring this year and this was her last hurrah before leaving UC. She doesn't care what happens to her—she just wants you to go down."

"Down?" I was shocked. "What did I do to her?"

"There's a bunch of folks that are foaming at the mouth over this thing with Beverly," my friend told me. "They think you're weak now, and they want someone else to take over. Ireta's retiring and is campaigning for Josephine Hammer, Ireta's good friend, to replace you. Ireta's got a big mouth and has ripped you to shreds up and down the state." I wasn't too surprised by this. "Be careful. Watch your back," and she quickly said good-bye.

I sent an email to Frank that I'd heard about a petition circulating to remove me from office. He replied that the dean's office had just seen the letter, and I had a right to receive a copy of it.

Percy faxed the letter, dated February 23, 2007, to my home on March 2, 2007. I was now aware that Ireta had been friendly to me for a reason; like Fred, she was fishing for information.

The three-page letter was a petition with twenty academic names typed at the end. [9] There weren't any signatures, although Ireta's name was identified as the author and was first on the list. Number twenty-one, at the end, was "anonymous" just like Angela had said.

I noted Angela's supervisor's name on the letter! *Oh, my god, no wonder she was so nervous!*

The other names were people I'd worked with for years and considered them to be good friends. There were also five names I didn't recognize at all. *Who are these people?* I wondered.

> Dear Dr. Grossman,
>
> The following statement presents the independent opinions and sentiments of the individuals listed below ... We, the undersigned ... call upon you to remove Amy Block Joy from the position of ... Director. We respectfully request that your interim replacement be ... [from] individuals listed below.

As Angela suggested, someone on the list wanted my job. Number two on the list—Josephine, a young, highly competitive academic—had already made claims to wanting my job before. Not very discreet, she was openly vying for my job. I'd respected her, thought she was talented and creative, but now, my opinion had changed. She was stooping low. The letter contained a number of allegations related to the investigation. It was poorly written and disorganized. The major topics were heavily spiced up with gossip.

> The reasons are clear. The tactics used by Dr. Joy have ... lack of leadership ... understanding ... sensitivity ... The blatant mismanagement ... has resulted in ... audits ... We have not had a respectful and effective relationship with Amy ... abandoned and abdicated ... to [Beverly] ... resulted in rampant misuse of ... funds ...

The first two pages blamed me for Beverly's fraud. "We believe ... staff morale has continued to decline ... this letter, therefore, is a formal communication of 'no confidence' and a request to replace Amy . . ."

The last two pages of the letter included a laundry list of trivial grievances, including not enough staff training, curriculum problems, and my personal favorite: "She distributed a brochure that did not reflect the high standards of the University . . ."

That brochure was developed by a committee composed of several people listed signing the letter, including the "anonymous" Patricia. I agreed that the brochure was lame—but that's what the committee wanted! Did they forget they developed the brochure?

The end of the letter contained a threat: "Should a change . . . not occur immediately, we the undersigned will reconsider whether we will submit a . . . budget for the next fiscal year . . . usually due in March."

I was disturbed that I couldn't defend myself. Frustrated, I hoped that the university would support me. I planned to face down my critics and tell them that their participation was voluntary, and I'd respectfully accept anyone's termination, preferring to work with those who were committed to the program.

After receiving and reading the fax around five in the afternoon, I called Percy at his home.

"Hi, Percy," I began, "it's Amy."

"Oh, hello. Did you get the fax?"

"Yes, thanks. I'm pretty sick about it," I said. After a short pause I asked, "Percy, I'd like to consult with someone about the letter. This isn't about the investigation, this is about retaliation. I know I can't talk about being cleared, but I need guidance on handling retaliation."

I actually had someone in mind that I wanted to talk to. I'd asked Percy a number of times but my request had been repeatedly denied. I hoped Percy would soften and change his mind.

"Oh, sure. That makes sense. Now, let's see who might you speak to? Let's think about this," he said thoughtfully.

I waited.

"Who'd be helpful in this sort of situation?" he continued

calmly. "I'd suggest maybe a therapist, a minister," he said.

"I'm Jewish," I reminded him.

"Oh, yeah, forgot, ahhh, a rabbi."

I had the feeling he was avoiding suggesting that I speak to a lawyer and was quickly running out of ideas.

"Percy, how about a neighbor?"

"A neighbor?" he said sounding confused. I waited.

"Sure," he said, kind of chuckling at the idea, then added, "as long as your neighbor doesn't work for UC."

"Don't worry," I said, "I wasn't planning on knocking on the door of President Dynes!" The university president's residence was at the end of my street in Kensington.

"Good," he said, still puzzled.

I thanked him and said good-bye.

I ran across the street clutching the letter and knocked on the door of my neighbor. Daniel Ellsberg opened the door. After exchanging a neighborly hello, I announced that I was a whistleblower. He immediately invited me into his kitchen.

I had met Daniel years ago when his wife, Patricia, and I worked on earthquake preparedness for our neighborhood. I highly admired him for his courage and integrity in releasing the information that helped lead to the end of the war in Vietnam, and I considered him to be the most famous whistleblower of all time. Recently, I'd brought a friend who was running for our town's police board to meet Daniel, and we had all had dinner together. I'd not told anyone about my whistleblower report, in accordance with the university's restrictions to keep a lid on it.

"Tell me everything," he began as I sat down by the big window overlooking their manicured front entrance. On the table was a pile of papers he had been working on. He pushed them aside to make elbow room. Lovely, fragrant flowers were in a vase on the table next to me.

We spoke elbow to elbow for almost two hours.

"I work for UC Davis. I found embezzlement and confronted my employee in front of the departmental chair, who told me it was no big deal. I think he's involved, maybe even in a cover-up, and I've heard recently about kickbacks. I met with the police and federal agents ..." The story poured out of me.

"And now, some of my friends, my colleagues, people who attended my wedding, people whom I wrote letters of recommendation for, now they want to remove me. Here's their petition." I unfolded the fax.

"Yes," Daniel told me. "This is all a form of retaliation, and it's against the law.

"This letter contains their names," he said as he looked down the list of the typed names. "Typically an organization will try to get rid of the truth seeker by keeping you unbalanced and distracted. You must not be dissuaded from the job ahead by attempts to harass or disturb you."

Daniel told me about his experience and the road ahead for me. "Most likely, you'll not regret what you did, but your life will be different. Friendships you took for granted may tragically end, and people you cared about will abandon and betray you. It's better to know and prepare for these things.

"Worse, you'll suffer for being a truth seeker. It's going to get harder. But don't despair when your friends desert you. All of it is unfortunate and irreversible. You'll be tested and re-tested, and they'll try to break you. You'll need to find new friends and build a new life."

He continued. "This isn't an experience that one bounces back from. This is a future-altering event that will change your view of the world forever. Be careful, things can turn ugly unexpectedly."

Hearing him speak so calmly and confidently, I felt comforted. I'd already read these things, but having someone, someone who's been there, tell me made a big difference. I found his complete honesty to be a great relief and very validating.

Daniel was my hero, and I wanted to be just like him.

"Few people will understand what you feel," he said, and I hugged him. "But remember, it's you that will sleep better knowing you did the right thing. Accept your new life now and try to embrace it as an opportunity."

"Thank you," I said with tears in my eyes. He handed me a copy of his book, *Secrets*, and signed it, *Amy, For truth and justice. Daniel Ellsberg.* [10]

I interviewed a couple of colleagues not listed on the petition, and they gave me permission to talk about their experience with the letter's author. Isabel Cisneros, in San Bernardino County, and Lupe Ramos, in Santa Cruz County, both reported feeling pressured to sign it. Isabel told me she never actually saw the letter but was asked to sign it via a telephone call. She indicated it was read out loud to her and the person reading it wouldn't give her a copy.

I drafted a response for Percy. We met, and he suggested that we adopt a wait-and-see approach, giving me the impression that this petition didn't constitute an official university action. "This is really the opinion of a bunch of rambunctious folks. Let me talk to some people. There's nothing to panic about," he calmly told me. Considering that the letter was addressed to him and not me, I relaxed and expected that he'd manage any fallout.

It was going to be awkward working with people who were angry and misguided. I became convinced that the biggest show of strength would be to get another year of funding without these folks. I moved full steam ahead, recalling Daniel Ellsberg's advice to stay the course. I became doggedly determined to succeed, gambling on Percy's efforts to dispel the group's unruliness.

The drama finally unfolded on Thursday, March 15, 2007, when the Justice Department posted a news release covering the U.S. Attorney's indictment against Beverly Benford.

The news release included a Department of Justice gold seal.

Sacramento Woman Indicted for Theft of
Government Property (March 15, 2007)
SACRAMENTO – United States Attor-

ney McGregor W. Scott announced today
that a federal grand jury returned a one-count
indictment charging Beverly Benford, of Sacramento, with theft of government property.
    This case is a product of an investigation by
the United States Department of Agriculture.
    According to Assistant United States Attor-
ney R. Steven Lapham, who is prosecuting the
case, the indictment alleges that Benford mis-
appropriated federal funds while an employee
at the University of California, Davis. The
funds came from the $13.3 million annual . . .
Program that Benford administered. Benford
is alleged to have made fraudulent purchases
and travel expense claims over a period of at
least six years . . .
    The misappropriation of funds was initially
reported to the University of California, Davis
officials in August, 2006, as a whistleblower
complaint . . . Benford has resigned her position... The maximum statutory penalty for a
violation of Section 641 is ten years, a fine of
$250,000, and a three year term of supervised
release . . .

Ginny and I printed a color copy and handed it to Ryan.
"Ten years in prison!" Ryan exclaimed.
"That's the maximum," I said. "She probably won't get the
maximum sentence since this is her first offense."
"What if she gets off? Who's this Prosecutor Lapham? Is he
any good?" Ginny suddenly looked worried. Ryan got on his
computer to Google him. I'd already done so.
"I've heard he's good, or if you really want to know ask the
Unabomber," I said matter-of-factly.
"What!" All eyes turned to me and I broke into a big grin.
"Don't worry—she's toast!"

Ryan found Attorney Lapham on the web and sure enough there were plenty of articles and photos on his successful prosecution of the Unabomber. We all felt giddy breathing a big sigh of relief. Ryan suddenly cautioned us.

"She's not behind bars, yet."

The next day, Friday, March 16, 2007, the front page of the *Sacramento Bee* carried the headline, "UCD Worker Accused of Theft." The byline was Carrie Peyton Dahlberg, the reporter I'd spoken to on February 21. Her story was well-written and insightful.

> A former UC Davis employee was indicted Thursday on one count of theft of government property, in a case that raises broader questions about how the university handled money for teaching the poorest Californians . . . The woman, Beverly Benford, 65, of Sacramento, is suspected of a six-year spree of submitting fake travel expenses and buying consumer electronics . . . according to court documents. The losses could total about $160,000, said U.S. Attorney, McGregor Scott. In addition, UC Davis officials said they continue to investigate . . . allegations that a campus department may have benefited improperly from large amounts of federal funds . . .

The rest of the article was on page A15. The article described the program's purpose and quoted a number of UC officials.

> Benford told the *Bee* last week that she could not comment on any specifics before consulting with a lawyer, but that in general all expenditures made by the program were approved by its director, Block Joy.

Yet it was Block Joy who filed a whistleblower complaint with the university, asking
that the funding irregularities be investigated,
according to a preliminary document which
was given to the *Bee* by a law enforcement
source in Yolo County.

The campus police officer who prepared the
document and is not identified by name wrote
that Block Joy told him she used the whistleblower system because "she felt her concerns
with Benford's theft of grant funds would go
unaddressed."

Benford bought iPods, DVD players, computers, expensive TVs, cameras and PDAs . . .
not allowed under the program.

The earlier campus police document said
that Block Joy first became concerned with
Benford's activities in September 2005, when
Benford canceled a trip after being paid a
$1,000 travel advance.

As Block Joy began examining records,
more irregularities emerged, it said, including
a camcorder and a home stereo system . . . that
Benford acknowledged were at her home.

Block Joy confronted Benford in the presence of [Food, Health and Society] Department chairman [Raymond Savage] over the
camcorder in March 2006 . . . Benford . . .
wrote a letter of apology and a check to pay
for the camcorder, but as more trouble was
found, Block Joy became frustrated by the lack
of official response . . . At one point . . . Block
Joy theorized to campus police that Benford
was being shielded by higher-ups because she
helped others obtain equipment improperly
. . . The officer wrote that the theory seemed

to be consistent with a spreadsheet detailing
nine years of program equipment purchases . . .
$798,826.

. . . UC Davis' Internal Audit Services . .
. advised . . . that there was a potential that
some of the merchandise purchased by Benford, such as computers and other electronic
equipment, is actually being used in the UC
Davis...[Food, Health and Society] department . . . misappropriation of grant funds.

[Savage] who heads the . . . department said
he couldn't comment . . . Block Joy refused to
discuss the allegations.

The alleged misuse . . . was outlined in a
document drawn up by campus police to prepare to ask a judge for permission to search
the employee's office cubicle and home. That
document was never filed, and an affidavit for
search warrant, prepared in October by . . . a
special agent for the U.S. Department of Agriculture's Office of Inspector General . . .

In asking permission . . . affidavit focused
only on Benford, outlining her purchase
records, emails . . . discuss[ing] Craig list ads
. . . Benford was giving away some items and
selling others.

Benford . . . to be arraigned on April 5 in
federal court . . . retired with a lump sum pension "cash out" of $268,688.

The university cannot withhold or delay a
pension payment to anyone under investigation for stealing government funds, because
employees have a right to the pensions that
they earned, said . . . vice-chancellor for human
resources.

After reading the article many times, I finally believed that the secrecy was over, and I could shout from the rooftops. Elated, I bought twenty-five copies of the paper and rushed home to spread the news. First, I told Judith, who was shocked and surprised. She knew Beverly and just couldn't believe it.

"She embezzled money from the poor!"

When she saw the part about my being a whistleblower she said, "I'm proud of you, Mom."

I invited my liberal Berkeley buddies over for tea and gave them each a newspaper to read without giving them a hint about the story. They seemed not to get it, asking a million questions. Finally one of them said to me, "You must be quite stressed."

Another friend met me at a coffee shop. She got it immediately. "Scumbag," was all she said.

The *Sac Bee* article was picked up by the Associated Press and this released a chain of new articles up and down California and across the nation. Widely distributed as a cautionary tale to an idyllic university fable, the *Sac Bee* article created a dialogue among my counterparts in other states. I was on the national list-serve so was privy to blog discussions from academics all over the United States. It was weird reading opinions from people I'd known for years.

The main response was fear. People in other universities worried about the ripple effect. Would programs be audited? Would the rules become stricter? Would the paperwork become more demanding? Although a couple of people commented that it was good that the crime was exposed, the majority of responses were, "Now things are going to be more difficult for everyone!"

I printed out ten articles that day that appeared in newspapers from Los Angeles to North Dakota. In fact, Ginny told me the story was on the evening news in Sacramento.

The *Sac Bee* article also rocked the boat in Davis. People started dropping like flies.

Fred was the first casuality. Five days later on March 21, he laid it out in black and white. His email was widely distributed.

> I am writing as a follow-up to our last faculty meeting and the obvious need to move a number of things forward. First, I have been asked to step down as of July 1 . . . this was not my plan . . . As you might guess, much of this has to do with the current investigation for which the indictment is sufficiently serious . . .

Many folks who were closely linked to Beverly and Raymond rushed in to console him. In my mind, I pictured poor Fred with Beverly's sword piercing his loyal old heart.

The second casualty was a bigger surprise. At the end of March, I received a rather curt email from my colleague Darci. She'd been avoiding me for months. Her unfriendly email contained a lengthy resignation letter from one of her staff, Felix Mercer, which she copied to the dean's office.

Felix resigned on March 29. He'd worked for Darci and blamed me for his sudden departure. His one-page diatribe included, "I am personally and professionally offended and embarrassed by events . . . Sac Bee . . . questioned about my role . . . I no longer want to be funded by the . . . program or be part of a program that is under Dr. Amy Joy."

I was saddened and frustrated that there was nothing I could do or say. I requested to meet with Darci and Felix, and I received a hostile retort.

However, when Felix turned in his equipment a week later, one of the items he returned was a Pocket PC, a piece of equipment that I'd not approved. This item was an inappropriate purchase by Beverly. *Did Felix receive one of Beverly's gifts? Is this what Fred meant by kickbacks?* I fully believed that Darci was aware of what Beverly was doing. I recalled her defense of Beverly when she accused me of mistreating her.

Darci immediately put in paperwork to terminate her staff appointment with our food stamp program and used another funding source, most likely from Raymond, to pay their salary. To me this signaled a need for her to clean house. Whether she was involved or, like Felix, a feckless victim, she definitely wanted out.

On Saturday, April 7, 2007, Fred launched his attack. Daniel Ellsberg had warned me to be prepared that those who were most affected would be full of anger. Fred was seething.

Fred sent me a very long and rambling email, copied to Percy and others at the dean's office. He actually sent the email three times, each time forgetting an attachment or correcting typos. He also forgot to mark the email confidential. I received it when I arrived at work on Monday morning.

Amy,

The following outlines several requests . . . a serious concern.

I am aware that there was a meeting on Friday . . . budget proposal . . . information was available on April 6 and not available today . . . In the section . . . you . . . identify a "Nutrition Education Training" of $150,000 with little detail and of particular concern a "Nutrition Education for Adult and Youth" . . . $127,075 . . . my concerns should be obvious . . . you have obligated. . . Raymond, Darci, and I. . . (without our knowledge or detailed discussion) to a commitment equivalent to $250,000 . . . Why didn't you let us know?

Fred had Googled and located on the Web an "old" budget of Beverly's. He'd forgotten that he was in charge of the program and that we had finalized the budget by removing those "obligations" that he was concerned about. However, at the time, and even now, I couldn't reveal to Fred that Raymond's lame claim that he was doing $250,000 worth of "nutrition education training" wasn't legit. The misappropriation was still under investigation, and I didn't want to tip Raymond off.

If I hadn't been so upset, I might have doubled over laughing. Fred was agreeing with me, although he wasn't aware of it!

Fred continued, "You have to know that in addition to the Federal case, because of inferences made in the police report and . . . allegations, there has been an ongoing audit of the department's records and a very serious UCD-015-Procedures for Faculty Misconduct Allegation."

Fred's inclusion of the Faculty Misconduct Allegation meant that Raymond was under investigation, explaining why his computer was taken. Fred, not good with secrets, had let the cat out of the bag!

And he continued.

"Accordingly I am asking you immediately to: Justify . . . why you . . . thought involving Raymond, Darci, and I was appropriate?"

Fred then rambled on, making unclear points about fund sources I didn't know about, including a shoe company that provided gift funds to Raymond's account. This in turn created a new audit with Fred and others getting into more hot water.

> 5. Also, if the misconduct case goes forward
> be prepared to provide emails, detailed bud-
> get notes, and related information so that any
> of your colleagues who may be affected will
> be able to comment or develop a defense as
> needed . . . you have to appreciate that many of
> us have been affected by all of this. In fact, the
> dean stated publicly in the last faculty meeting
> that my service as interim chair will end on
> July 1 . . . This was not my plan . . .

The idea that I might have to give documents to Fred was unnerving. I sent the email to the auditors to find out. They told me that all requests for investigative documents would be handled by the LDO.

I wasn't going to be bullied. I replied the same day.

> Dear Dr. Stone,
>
> Thank you for your email. First, you are not committed . . . Second, I will post the Amendment (once approved) . . . as is the usual practice . . . on our Web site . . . Third, regarding your other questions, I am not in the position to respond at this time due to the investigations.
> Sincerely,
> Amy Block Joy, Director

Fred wasn't happy and sent me a response the next day.

> Your response is hardly satisfying . . . In addition to me, Raymond, Darci, and the department will need clarification beyond an email that we have no obligations. All of us view this as a serious matter. If you or your staff made some kind of error so be it . . . also appreciate, those who have to respond to . . . related investigations have rights to materials . . . needed for a defense.

His irate reply allowed me to request that someone at the dean's office talk to him on my behalf.

This email discussion marked the end of all communication with Fred.

Early April, Judith received exciting news. She was accepted at UCLA for fall 2007. She called Jake and found out that he had gotten into Dartmouth. I was very pleased that Judith was going to attend the University of California, like I had. UCLA seemed to me to be a perfect fit!

On April 19, I received another interview request. The editorial director of the Pacific Research Institute for Public Policy, K. Lloyd Billingsley, was writing a column about Beverly for a Sacramento journal, *Capital Ideas*. I passed on his questions and my draft responses to vice-chancellor for communications, Elizabeth Pritchard. Elizabeth guided me on ways to provide factual information in a positive context, including the impact of our national nutrition program. On April 24, he wrote "Food for Fraud," two pages on Beverly's embezzlement. [11]

> Authorities here are charging Beverly Benford . . . with embezzling funds by means of false purchases . . . Beverly has pleaded not guilty . . . this program, in its own description, exists to "improve the likelihood . . . eligible for [food stamps] will make healthy food choices within a limited budget . . . In other words, put down those nachos, pick up your veggies . . . UC Davis nutritionist Amy Block Joy, says that every dollar spent on the nutrition . . . saves . . . health care costs . . . Meanwhile, the alleged embezzler Beverly Benford . . . faces a maximum penalty of 10 years in prison, a $250,000 fine, and three years of supervised release. In court she will face Steven R. Lapham . . . who prosecuted Theodore Kaczynski, also known as the Unabomber . . . Lapham gained a conviction in the Unabomber case.

On Friday, May 11, 2007, at an afternoon retirement party

at the Faculty Club for Dr. Jonas Markos, I found a friendly face. Dr. Markos, a witty political intellectual, was internationally famous for his work on Vitamin D. He was highly regarded academically and loved by everyone in the department.

I'd been standing alone at the drinks table, when a faculty member from a neighboring department, Dr. Matt Sorenson, smiled and came over to say hello. Matt, a developmental biochemist from Columbia University Medical School, was, at age forty-three, one of the youngest members of the faculty to become a lifetime member in the Academy of Biological Sciences. Matt, tall and lanky with wavy sandy-blond hair, cobalt blue eyes, and a neatly trimmed beard, asked how I was doing.

"Not bad," I answered and held up my glass of champagne.

"And how are you, Matt?" I asked, glancing around to see if Raymond had arrived.

"I'm good," he said. "By the way, Fred told me that you're raking in the bucks with this thing about Beverly."

"Huh?" I said.

"Some sort of monetary award for blowing the whistle," Matt told me.

"Oh, that's totally untrue. I didn't receive any award, monetary or otherwise, from blowing the whistle," I said downing the glass and looking around for another. "Unless you consider harassment and hostility rewarding."

"So, what's it like being a whistleblower?" Matt asked.

"Piece of cake," I said eyeing the desserts. "Oh you mean, how's life in the fast lane? Well, let me put it this way," I said, looking around first to see who might be eavesdropping, "I'd not recommend it for the faint of heart."

Matt had heard my jokes before and shared my sense of humor. He shared some gossip that I hadn't heard.

"Raymond's been doing this sort of 'helping the department' for a long time!"

"Really? Tell me more," I said intrigued.

"Well, let's start with all the people he's hired. First, there's Darci, then there's all the others."

"He hired Darci?" I gasped.

"Oh yeah. Haven't you seen all their publications together? She was his protégée." Matt added, "Don't you think that he's, well, kind of, ah, full of himself?"

Out of the corner of my eye I saw Fred in the distance, stuffing his face with food while chatting with the guest of honor.

We both turned silently to glance over at Raymond, who was talking animatedly with a group of giggling graduate students, all female and looking star-struck.

"OK, Matt," I said whispering, "here's the million-dollar question."

Matt's eyes got big.

"Any hanky-panky between Raymond and Beverly?" I asked, looking directly at him to see if my question jarred him in any way. I'd hoped to put an end to the speculations and all the questions I'd been asked over and over again.

Matt burst into laughter, spewing his champagne.

"Yuck," he said, finishing with a conclusive "no way." I believed this was true. I saw a twinkle in his eye as though he was about to tell me something interesting, but we were suddenly interrupted.

Fred waltzed by on his way toward Raymond and the pretty graduate students.

"Did Fred tell you about his brush with the law?" I asked Matt.

"So many times . . ." he said, shaking his head.

"I don't get it," I added. "He should be embarrassed, not bragging. Should I tell him: Good for you, Fred—now get a life!" I paused, still watching Fred, who was now laughing with Raymond.

"I did feel sorry for him," I admitted as I observed Darci and her own entourage skipping over to Raymond, now surrounded by his groupies.

"Big mistake!" Matt cautioned me. I finished another glass of champagne, and the party began to hum. Saying good-bye to Matt, I weaved over to congratulate the retiree before he joined

Raymond's fan club.

Walking back to my office a little tipsy, I was happy that I'd attended. At least, I wasn't intimidated. And now, with Matt, there was someone to talk to.

Matt and I became telephone buddies. I'd often call him to find out about faculty meetings, especially what Fred was telling people. He told me that Fred went on the defensive telling folks that I filed the whistleblower report to protect "my own backside."

Although unnerved by this inaccurate, untrue malicious gossip, all I could do was let it go. After all, the faculty were smart people and they'd eventually see the truth. People had already begun avoiding me by canceling meetings, not returning telephone calls or responding to emails, just as Daniel Ellsberg had predicted. The one advantage this offered was that it freed me to do all the paperwork that was beginning to become tiresome and exhausting.

I began to arrange conference calls rather than attend meetings. My phone rarely rang now that the word was out about the investigation. I was just going to concentrate on the things that really mattered while I waited out the brewing storm.

On May 24, 2007, I attended a USDA nutrition meeting. I was a little nervous because I wasn't sure how they felt about Beverly, whom many had known personally. I wasn't planning on bringing the subject up, but it was constantly on my mind.

The meeting was ordinary. No one mentioned the investigation, and all the people who attended were friendly. In fact, I felt like I'd returned to my former life where the major topics of casual, nonprofessional conversation were our children.

After the meeting I bumped into one of the USDA dignitaries, who walked up to me and said, "I want to shake your hand."

I'd known Walter for many years and although we'd only spoken about food stamps statistics, I'd always admired him from
a distance.

I shook his hand. He said, "Thank you for what you've done
for the U.S. Department of Agriculture. It was courageous of
you to step forward."

I almost burst into tears hearing his praise.

"Thank you. It means a lot to me to hear you say this,"
I said as we stood there shaking hands. A group of people
had joined us.

He went on to tell me that they'd heard about the warrant
and that the USDA was pleased that the university was stepping up to the plate.

"Yes, there are many good people at the university," I replied.
"You know that this thing with Beverly was very unique," and
stopped, worried that I might say too much.

"We're on the same page," he said. Many of the USDA folks
that I'd worked with over the years had gone to UC Davis or
sent their kids there. One of the high-level officials was even
the brother of a former Davis mayor. We stood there in silence
reflecting on the need to maintain high standards.

"Thank you for your support," was all I said as we both went
our separate ways.

I returned to Davis after the meeting and bumped into Raymond. I was leaving the parking lot, headed back to my office,
and he was on his way to his car. I hadn't seen him up close in
ages, mostly because my office was on the first floor and his was
on the third.

Raymond was carrying some of his office artifacts. I assumed
he must be moving out. I felt I was ready to greet him.

As he approached, I walked confidently toward him. As we
got closer I looked him in the eye and said cheerfully, "Hi Raymond, how are you?", smiling.

He turned his head away and looked down, saying nothing. I
noticed that he'd gained weight and looked downtrodden.

Matt called and gave me the scoop about Fred. Matt said that Fred was in the mail room openly discussing a letter that Raymond had received. Fred said that Ray was being investigated for misconduct by the university's chancellor's office, and it was so serious that he'd hired a lawyer.

"It's an ethics violation," Matt said, "and the word around the department is that you fingered him. Everyone knows," he concluded.

I didn't respond, not really knowing what to say. I was keenly aware of what this might mean for Raymond's future. As Fred had already told me in his April email to several folks at the dean's office and in the department, Raymond was being accused of faculty misconduct.

On June 15 Judith graduated! I had a party for her, which was attended by many friends, most of whom also had daughters going off to college. Then she left for a ten-day vacation in Mexico with several of her girlfriends.

From mid-June to September, I worked like a dog to get the program approved for another year of funding. The USDA required more details than ever, and preparing the contract and then revising it three times was a lot of work.

The twenty people from the no-confidence petition all changed their minds and turned in budgets on the due date. In fact, even Patricia, the anonymous twenty-first name, was leading the pack and requesting a large amount of funding.

Rebecca provided the essential back-up support for the budget. She was exhausted by the constant revisions, and I was worried she'd quit. But we managed to pull it off in the end. The dean's office provided a structure for the budget to withstand the USDA's tight scrutiny. Our final submission was nearly three hundred pages.

In early September I drove Judith down to begin her college adventure at UCLA. It was fun moving her into the dorm. We hung out for a few days, visiting the Santa Monica beach and going to the Getty and other museums. A number of friends were there with her, and it was an easy transition. I was thrilled that she was on her way to something fun and exciting.

On September 30, 2007, I received a letter approving our program for $13 million. We were rewarded for the hard work, and I was greatly relieved that our program would continue under the watchful eyes of the dean's office. My next task, which was a federal requirement and a big job, was to prepare the final report on our program accomplishments from the previous year.

On November 19 the audit report was released to the public in the form of a UC press release. We were nervous. The forty-page document contained a report on Beverly and her embezzlement and fraud, a report on the nutrition department allegations, and a controls report.

I met with the auditors who'd briefed me prior to the release. Stephen Grant, director of Internal Auditing Services (IAS), went over the major findings. The *Sac Bee* had made a public request of the information and the university prepared for the onslaught. A strict and rigorous control system and more training had corrected many of the failures that the auditors had identified.

On November 20 the *Sacramento Bee* published another front-page story, "Misuse Found in UCD Funds" by reporter Carrie Peyton Dahlberg.

> A federal program aimed at teaching the poorest Californians how to eat right was misused by the UCD nutrition department, paying for computers, remodeling and unrelated research, campus auditors said in a report released Monday.
> Three heavily censored audits . . . released by

the university in response to a *Sacramento Bee*
public records request found that . . . $2.3 mil-
lion in fiscal year 2005–2006 alone—dwarfs
the $160,000 estimate made in March when a
former . . . employee was indicted for . . . theft
of government property.

One atypical example . . . Program paid for
research promoted by [food maker EQUI-
NOX] . . . included in that amount is $200,000
that the university is attributing to Beverly
Benford . . . however, instances in which the
. . . program paid for things it shouldn't have,
include:

• $80,522 in salaries and benefits for two
researchers who worked for former departmental chairman [Raymond Savage], one of
them an EQUINOX-related project.

• $11,497 to renovate a conference room,
adding media capabilities.

• $101,291 that went largely for computer
servers and computers for the university's
nutrition department.

The audit also found that . . . program
"intentionally misstated" spending in a budget
. . . "disguised" because it wouldn't have been
approved otherwise.

The visible portions of the audit do not
name . . . chairman of the department. . .
Instead, using the title of former departmental
chairman the audit states that his "failure to
act on allegations of fraud" allowed abuses by
one employee to continue . . . It details a 2005
episode in which the identity of an employee
who made a fraud allegation became known,
leading to a confrontation between the accuser
and a relative of the accused. The accuser

promptly resigned, generating fear in the
department that others who reported impro-
prieties could lose their jobs, the audit said.

As before, the news story was picked up by the Associated
Press and was widely reported on up and down California.
The UCD campus newspaper, the *California Aggie*, published
a similar article by reporter Cameron Mortimer on Wednesday,
November 28.

> University Concludes Internal Investiga-
> tion: Allegations of Theft and Fraud Lead to
> Criminal Charges
> After three separate audits, UC Davis' Inter-
> nal Audit Services concluded in a November
> 19 press release . . . The U.S. Department of
> Agriculture provides funding for the program
> . . . Following a whistleblower's report of mal-
> feasance in August 2006, UC Davis officials'
> subsequent investigation revealed that fraud
> had indeed been committed. These findings
> were the reported to the USDA, which in
> conjunction with the U.S. Attorney's Office,
> formally began a criminal investigation in
> October, culminating with the indictment
> of Beverly Benford in March. Benford who
> resigned . . . is charged with theft totaling
> nearly $200,000...Fund were misappropri-
> ated . . . from travel . . . to electronic devices . . .
> resold on the internet . . .

With all the negative attention generated by the articles,
I again began to be seriously concerned about retaliation. I
avoided going upstairs to the third floor to pick up my mail after
finding some opened and torn as well as some strange drawings
on certain envelopes. I stopped attending faculty meetings.

Matt told me that Fred was bitter now that he was essentially a lame duck. Raymond wasn't around. I kept a low profile mainly because I wasn't keen on being associated with these people.

However, I did have a job to do and getting folks to provide their accomplishment data was like pulling teeth. By copying the dean's office on my requests, I managed to get people's attention, and the reports started rolling in.

On Thursday, December 13, I'd nearly completed our final report on the health improvements of the 110,000 food stamp families we served in 2006. In the report I included my results from the cost-benefit study that documented medical cost savings from nutrition education. I felt satisfied and pleased that our results showed that the program was helping families improve their eating habits. I was ready to close the books on another successful year.

However, even though the program was humming along, I wasn't feeling that great. Initially, I thought I was just run down.

That afternoon, after receiving a phone call from a colleague telling me that the gossip vine was spreading rumors that I was mentally ill, I went outside to unwind. My heart was racing. I thought the discomfort would go away with some fresh air and a change of scene, but after another hour of palpitations, it was hard to ignore.

I called my doctor in Berkeley at four-thirty in the afternoon, and his receptionist put me on hold. As I waited on the telephone, I wrote down my symptoms: irregular pulse 100, pain in jaw, dizziness, clammy.

"Dr. Marks," his familiar deep voice resonated.

"Dr. Marks, thanks for taking my call. I'm at work in Davis and am having heart palpitations. My pulse is rapid and irregular. I'm also a little dizzy," I said straightforwardly.

"How long have you had these symptoms?" he asked.

"About an hour, although I've felt crummy all afternoon."

"You need to get to the ER and have this checked out,"

he said.

I called Ginny to my office and asked if she'd take me to Summit Hospital. I downplayed my symptoms. She nodded and left to get her purse. I printed out the driving directions.

After five minutes, I wondered what happened to Ginny and called her. Her phone went directly to voicemail. Not feeling well enough to get up, I called Ryan, getting up only to open my door.

He popped his head inside the door.

"Ryan, could you find Ginny for me?" I said.

"Oh, my god," he said, "you're white as a ghost."

"Don't worry—I'm fine. But where's Ginny? She was going to take me to get this thing checked out."

Ryan ran to fetch her.

Ginny walked in. "I've called 911," she told me looking serious. "You're sweating profusely and don't look good. You need help now." In the distance I heard the sound of the ambulance. I was hardly feeling well enough to be startled. The whole world seemed surreal.

I sent a very short email to Franklin. "Ginny called 911."

The medics arrived as I hit the send button. Three of them went to work on me. One of them placed an oxygen mask over my mouth, as another medic rolled up my sleeve and took blood. A third medic hooked up electrodes to take an EKG. I answered some simple questions about the date and the name of the president, my name and telephone number, and then some medical questions about medications and allergic reactions. In less than three minutes, I was placed on a stretcher, some baby aspirin was put in my mouth, and I was asked to chew it. It was cherry flavored and bitter.

I marveled at how many people could fit in my office at the same time. There were three paramedics with a stretcher and a policeman standing a few feet in the hallway by my door. The sirens were blasting away as I visualized my career plummeting to the ground.

My blood pressure was 200/120. They put me into the ambulance and we drove away to nearby Sutter Hospital. Ginny followed the ambulance and brought my purse.

As I sat in the ambulance the policeman said he heard I was the whistleblower, and he would see me at the hospital.

In the ambulance I chatted with the medics. My irregular heartbeat was up to 120. They gave me a nitroglycerin pill under my tongue, and the pain in my jaw was instantly gone. The monitor in the ambulance displayed a number of irregular heartbeats, which I could readily feel as the sirens blared en route to the hospital.

I was kept at the hospital, and they said they wouldn't release me until my cardiac enzymes showed no muscle damage after two, four, and six hours. An assortment of tests were done, including a constant monitoring of blood pressure, EKG, chest X-ray, lung ultrasound, and blood work every hour. It took several hours for my blood pressure to come down. I stayed until one in the morning.

While waiting for the last enzyme test to show I was stable, I realized that I'd accomplished everything I wanted for the program and it was time to leave my position as director.

"Ginny," I said to her from my hospital bed, "I think it's time for me to go." Ginny stood up and reminded me that I hadn't been released. I decided not to tell her that it wasn't my hospital stay that I was talking about.

A half hour later, the enzyme levels were stable and my blood pressure was reduced enough for the doctor to allow me to release myself from the hospital.

Ginny stayed by my side the whole time. I told her that I'd take a taxi to my car, but she insisted on being with me. She took me to my car and I drove home. I didn't share my thoughts with Ginny for I was afraid that she'd try to talk me out of it.

I was sad. Much of what I loved about the work was gone. I was relieved that the program hadn't closed and would continue now with another year's funding. It wasn't going to be easy to say good-bye, but now was the time to pass the baton.

At home I fell asleep, feeling at ease with my decision. Now, to get Davis to agree.

After another check-up by my Berkeley doctor and an echo-cardiogram, I was ready to return to work. My heart was fine, although I had episodic high blood pressure and was diagnosed with severe stress.

I received a reply from Frank to my "Ginny called 911" email:

> I'm very sorry to hear that you had to be taken to the hospital. I've heard today that you are all right—I certainly hope that is the case. Your visit to the hospital and . . . further allegations of retaliation, cause me great concern. The assistant vice-provost and I would like to meet with you…to discuss options for resolving this situation. Please call me anytime.

On Tuesday, December 18, 2007, I drove to Davis to meet with officials at the provost's office. It was time to move on. No question, this was the right thing to do. The words of Daniel Ellsberg kept running through my mind. *You'll need to find new friends and build a new life. Accept your new life now and embrace it as an opportunity.*

Even though I loved my work helping poor families, the investigation and all its spins-offs proved to be a big distraction. A new person would be able to invest all their energy on building up the program. I'd accomplished two more years of funding after alerting the university to fraud. I was ready to let go.

Frank and Assistant Vice-Provost Eloise Summers met with me at nine o'clock.

"We want you to be successful," Frank said quietly.

"Thank you," I replied. "I feel encouraged. I want to continue to contribute to the university. My whole career has been dedicated to UC. My father worked for UC. I'm a graduate of UCB. I've worked for UC now for twenty-eight years and my daughter now attends UCLA. I'm a big fan!"

Eloise nodded. "We have some ideas we'd like to share with you."

I was told that many of the retaliation events that I'd officially reported through letters and emails had been verified, and this was discussed with me during the meeting. They suggested that I lay low and stay away from the Food, Health and Society Department, and I agreed. A lot of money would have to be repaid to the USDA and some of it, by that department.

"Folks in the department are very angry," I said. "I agree it would be better for me to stay away."

"Unfortunately, the investigation isn't over so it's likely to get worse before it gets better," Frank told me, looking at Vice-Provost Summers. He indicated that the future of the program was also uncertain.

They offered me a "no-fault" administrative leave to prepare for a new position and location that would allow me to retain my faculty appointment and continue my work at UC. The no-fault clause meant that the leave would not count as time spent on sabbatical or study leave. Dean Fitzgerald would work with me on the details.

"This is a good idea," I said.

Delighted by my new-found freedom, I agreed to their offer to develop a new faculty career. This was an exciting opportunity to put Beverly, Raymond, and the whole investigation to rest, box it all up, and reinvent myself.

8 | Healing

On the afternoon of Wednesday, December 19, 2007, I drafted an agreement for my new position based on my discussions with Frank and the assistant vice-provost. Called a Memorandum of Understanding (MOU), this document was a legal and binding agreement with the university to provide funding and resources for my future at the university. The purpose of the MOU was to clarify my return to my full-time faculty position. On January 1, 2008, I would no longer be responsible for the administration or management of the food stamp nutrition program, and this MOU was my security of employment. Working with Dean Fitzpatrick on the details, we included an announcement of my new position, my salary and benefits, a new office, and support funds for my new position to be located far from the Food, Health and Society Department. My already approved "no-fault" leave of absence was also included.

I heard from Percy that the dean's office was going to appoint an interim director for my program to oversee the day-to-day work until a search committee hired my replacement. The permanent director position would require a lengthy national search, involving advertisements in nutrition journals and a job description circulated to universities all over the United States. The hiring process would take at least ten months after a search committee was appointed.

In the meantime, they asked Glenda Quinn, an efficiency expert, to step in and run the office. Glenda, I heard through the grapevine, had transformed the Department of Entomology with her tough-minded decisions. In fact, her former boss, Dr. Henry Hollinger, the retired chair of that department, was being considered as the interim replacement to oversee the program until a permanent director was hired.

Dr. Hollinger, or Hank as everyone called him, was well-known throughout Davis as an experienced executive and a friendly, talented scientist. During his heyday at Davis he received national awards and honors, and he was recently nominated to the exclusive National Association for the Academy of Sciences. I was relieved that the university had asked someone with gobs of experience and a friendly temperament.

On Thursday, December 20, I completed and submitted my last USDA Final Report. I had a few more tasks as director, but the majority of my programmatic responsibilities ended when I hit the send button for the final report.

I took Ginny and Ryan out to lunch to celebrate our last year together and to talk about how my move might affect them. I phoned Rebecca and left a message. I wanted to give her a heads up on the situation and reassure her that her work was valued.

"Let's raise our tea cups and celebrate our year without Beverly," I toasted with Ryan and Ginny at our favorite Chinese restaurant.

"It's been an honor working with you both." I felt my eyes getting moist when I added, "It's too hard to say good-bye, so let's toast to our continuing friendship."

Ginny, Ryan, and I all clanged our cups in harmony.

Ryan turned to me after my toast. "Don't be sad," he said smiling, "I have news to share. Guess who I saw at the Christmas recital last night?"

Ryan pulled out his cell phone and showed us a photo.

Ginny yelped, "Gadzooks—it's Beverly!"

"And hey, check this out," Ryan added, pulling out a "Home for Sale" advertisement from his back pocket.

"That's her house!" Ginny exclaimed.

"Let me see!" I said, grabbing the piece of paper. "Yikes," I said, pointing to another photo in the corner of the ad, "what's that in her kitchen?"

Ginny was cracking up. "That," she said laughing, "is the security surveillance monitor on top of her fridge!"

Ryan read the advertisement to us, mocking the flyer's exaggerations in his deep baritone voice. "This model home has a video security system."

I couldn't help myself. "The real estate agent left off the part that the security system had been seized by government agents."

"Bummer," chimed Ryan.

Ginny hummed the theme from *Twilight Zone.* "Buyer beware," she cautioned.

We laughed, maybe in part to dispel the underlying sense of how pathetic the whole thing was.

Later that afternoon, during an email discussion with Dean Fitzpatrick about the MOU, I was told that my salary would be reduced by $4,000! My director stipend of $333 a month would end on December 31, and this reduction in salary wasn't negotiable. I didn't sign the MOU, although I did complete everything I'd agreed to do.

At 5:28 p.m., on Friday, December 21, my last day as director, I sent my email announcement addressed to all my colleagues. It was short and sweet. "After discussions and consultation with the dean's office, I have accepted a new role . . . I wish everyone a peaceful holiday season . . . It's been an enriching experience . . . improving the health and nutrition of low-income families. Keep up the great work."

After turning off the light of my office, I whispered, "Adios, amigo," to the dark, empty room, and shut the door behind me. I didn't look back.

Later that evening I was glad to get a call from Rebecca.

I was concerned about the new director being supportive about Rebecca's telecommuting, and had left her a message to call me.

"Rebecca, thanks for calling," I began, after I heard her say hello. Rock music was blasting in the background.

"I'm sorry it took so long to get back to you," she said shouting over the music. "Hold on," her voice was trailing, "I'm moving to a quieter room."

"I called to give you a heads up about some changes," I began after the background noise subsided. "I don't know if you've heard but I'm returning to my academic position on January 1."

"I know," Rebecca admitted, sounding gloomy. "Glenda called me yesterday," she added. *News travels fast,* I thought.

"Did Glenda talk to you about your position?" I asked, worried.

"Not really," Rebecca said, "she just called to ask me to meet with her the first week in January. She mentioned that I'd be reporting to her as of January 1."

We spoke for forty-five minutes, mostly exchanging ideas for the year ahead and working our way to saying good-bye.

"Rebecca," I began, "this is just my recommendation, so take it with a pound of salt," I said now chuckling. "I recommend that you get the dean's office to put their approval for you to continue telecommuting in writing," I suggested. "They didn't mess with me about your telecommuting arrangement, knowing I'd fight them tooth and nail to keep you," I admitted, wondering if she was aware of the controversy.

If she was, she didn't say so. I shifted to a more intimate conversation about working together. It seemed a natural way to say good-bye now that I wasn't her supervisor.

"Rebecca, it's been great working with you and getting to know the real you. Unfortunately, Beverly kept us apart for many years," I opened up. "I was thinking about the first time I actually got to speak with you. It was at the office baby shower for Ryan and his wife in 2004, right?" I asked.

"Yes," she answered. "Ryan told me that Beverly never gave him the gift card." She paused. "I gave Beverly fifty bucks toward that gift!"

"Ditto," I said not wanting to reveal that I'd given one hundred. "I feel bad for Ryan."

"Beverly was always griping that she was broke," Rebecca told me, "but to steal their baby's money—grrrr." Rebecca was just getting warmed up.

"Did you have any idea that she was embezzling?" I asked, curious.

"Nope. Beverly was the boss from hell so I was always trying to placate her. She'd flatter me one day and scare me the next. She was all over the map. She knew I was dependent on keeping this job," Rebecca bristled.

"I keep wondering about if I missed any clues . . ." my voice fading as I heard a drum pounding in the background.

Rebecca spoke up. "Beverly made me think that you were a blathering idiot, forever changing your mind and making everyone jump through crazy hoops. She terrorized Ginny and tortured Ryan. With me, she was all sweet and friendly until the last six months. That's when she resorted to making threatening statements and making my life hell."

"Threatening?" I asked, wondering what Rebecca had told the auditors.

Rebecca then unleashed a torrent of emotion.

"Beverly guaranteed me a higher paying job then told me that you were going to fire me," Rebecca said nervously. "At the time, I was really vulnerable and believed her. She characterized you as the big, bad, crazed director, cursing you and telling me you were hostile and taking drugs to control your constant rage attacks."

She continued. "Beverly deceived and hurt all of us. She created a wall around you to make you appear unapproachable and intimidating, and she'd frequently remind us that Dr. Savage was in her corner," Rebecca said with her usual honesty.

"Rebecca, talking to you is helpful. I appreciate your candor," I said. "I want you to know that Beverly never spoke to me about you or your work. She didn't request a reclassification for your position and I never even thought of firing you."

Here was yet another side of Beverly that I hadn't come to terms with.

"You know, Rebecca, Beverly did all that to keep us from

communicating in order to cover up her criminal activity. She
needed you to work at home so that you and I wouldn't compare notes about what she was up to."

"Yep. I was her confidante," Rebecca groaned. "I think things
spun out of control when you started asking questions, challenging
her. And being a very jealous person, she wanted to destroy you."

"What was she jealous of?" I asked, curious.

"Your happiness, your success, your career, your future, your
fabulous husband, you name it."

"My fabulous husband?"

"Well, yes. Bev talked about your husband all the time. Being
the ambassador of England is quite distinguishing!"

I thought Rebecca was joking. "Ambassador? Are we still
talking about Leonard?" I said teasing her.

"Bev told everyone he was the ambassador," Rebecca replied
hesitantly.

"Huh?" was all I could say.

"Well," said Rebecca, her voice dropping, "he was always
traveling to foreign countries . . . and being British . . ." she said
then regained her usual composure. "Beverly wasn't telling the
truth was she?"

"No, Rebecca, Leonard isn't the British ambassador," I said. I
wondered what she would think if she knew how far from the
truth that really was.

Early the next Saturday morning, I invited Leonard to meet
me for breakfast at Fat Apples Restaurant in Berkeley. I'd been
giving him money to help him out over the years, especially
because of health concerns. But now I needed to let him know
that this was not going to continue.

At eight-thirty in the morning I arrived and found a table by
the window. I brought the *Sac Bee* article with me. It was time
for him to hear what had happened at UC Davis. Our relationship living separately and as co-parents and sort-of friends had
been mostly affable, although I was alarmed by his frequent
mood swings.

He'd been in a funk for the past year, oscillating between agreeable and belligerent. His health seemed to be deteriorating. He had severe migraines, dizziness, and had dropped ten pounds. After an extensive series of medical tests, nothing was found. His symptoms, or maybe his accounting of them, had gradually improved.

Financially, I was struggling. Leonard was contributing nothing to the house expenses or to Judith. I'd found a fixed loan which could have reduced the monthly mortgage payment, and I offered to split the monthly savings with him. He agreed, the bank arranged for the loan, and then at the last minute he refused to sign the papers, leaving me in the lurch to fork over five hundred dollars to cover the bank's "free" application fee!

Leonard arrived thirty minutes late and found me reading the paper at the table.

"How are you?" he asked, not even looking at me.

"Good," I said. "And you?"

He nodded as he sat down. He took off his glasses and wiped them with his handkerchief as he leaned back in his chair.

"I decided to walk here," he said, looking dignified and energetic.

This was his way of accounting for being late, although he must have forgotten that he told me two weeks ago that he'd sold his car.

"I want to share with you something that happened in Davis a while ago," I began. "Remember Beverly?"

"Beverly? Who's Beverly" he replied looking intently at the menu.

"Beverly, my program administrator, my budget person . . . You must remember her. She talked to you on the phone all the time," I said, trying not to sound irate.

"Nope, don't recall her at all."

"You do!" I almost shouted in protest. "Remember you called her my sidekick, and the two of you discussed the British education system in Jamaica. You got a kick out of her, impressed at her British upbringing." I paused, waiting to see some recognition.

"Nothing, nada, not even vague . . ." Still not looking at me, he asked, "Is the oatmeal any good here?" He motioned with his fingers for the waitress to come over.

"Leonard, Beverly embezzled money from the program, the food stamp program, and she's in serious trouble."

That got his attention. He was about to speak when the waitress arrived.

"I'd like the oatmeal without the brown sugar and a decaf coffee," Leonard told the waitress. I ordered a bran muffin and a café latte.

"You were saying something about Beverly . . ." he said. He was now looking at me.

Suddenly I changed my mind and forgot about Beverly.

"Leonard, let me give you the facts of life," I said assertively.

He raised his eyebrows at my provocative announcement. I finally had his full attention.

"The embezzlement caused a big ripple effect at the university. My salary was reduced. The bottom line—I can't provide any more money to you." I let that sink in. He looked dumbfounded and glum.

"I'll give you a check today, but it's the last one. It's going to be harder for me now. I'm getting a loan to pay for Judith's college," I added firmly. He was moving around uncomfortably in his chair.

"I need the money," he said angrily. "It's time for you to get out of the house and sell it," he said starting to threaten me.

I bristled at this; Leonard appeared to be doing well enough. Although not rolling in dough, his carefree and relaxed demeanor conveyed that he was unencumbered. Frequently bragging about some mission overseas, and the teaching job he had in Marin, he presented an economically secure lifestyle.

"You told me that things were going very well these days," I began, trying to change the subject.

"That teaching job across the bay, and your book," I reminded him. "You said you were getting an advance," I said trying not to make it sound like a question.

"Advance?" he repeated, his voice shrill. "Oh, no, no, no, no. The book's not ready," he stoutly denied the whole thing. "Here you go again, talking about money. Bloody hell, give it a rest," he finished, sounding cross. This was usually a signal that he assumed would shut me up. But not anymore. Instead, I pressed on.

"I'm not going to be able to support you now that Judith's in college," I declared putting my foot down.

The oatmeal arrived. He looked put-out and forlorn. We ate in silence.

When the bill arrived, I didn't offer to pay for him; instead, I deliberately put down my share of the bill in cash. Leonard reached into his pocket and sheepishly said, "I've left my wallet at my flat."

"How convenient," I said as I paid his share and got up to say good-bye, handing him a check. I smiled as I waved cheerio.

I was pleased that I'd stood up to him. I was relieved not to discuss Davis, or my trip to the ER and all the gory details. I didn't want to shock Sir Leonard, Ambassador of Kensington.

Surrounded by boxes I'd brought home from work, I was surprised how much I'd accumulated over the years. Now that the pressure of the grueling director job was over, I began the arduous task of reorganizing all my documents.

The firm Lester & Forbes (not actual name) was auditing years 2003 to 2005. I'd organized my documents by subject and they would need the information sorted by year. The large guest room of my home was filled to the brim with boxes. I began the task of re-sorting on Monday, January 14.

As I made my way through the records of my past, I numbered each box and summarized the contents. By Thursday, January 24, I had eighty boxes of evidence.

While sorting through personnel records, I pulled out the folder for Darci Small, my former so-called friend. Reading notes from meetings and projects, I confirmed that we clearly had a unique relationship. The kidding, the teasing, the clowning. It was a comic intimacy, boasting an intellectual banter.

Reading a card she gave me, I had to laugh. "Hey, let's put the fun back into dysfunctional"was the card's message. A glamorous cartoon-woman waving a magic wand glistened in shades of pink and red. Darci put my name next to the gorgeous gal, writing underneath my name, "That's you!"

I put the card back into the file and closed the box. *Well, the magic's gone now.*

I returned to the box of unsorted miscellaneous documents. Luckily, I could take back to my office this one and another ten boxes containing nutrition materials, publications, and program stuff.

I found boxes of field audits dated 1998 to 2005. I pulled out the file on Mendocino County and read the audit report I'd sent to Ireta Koskernof, the author of the petition to remove me. Having audited all forty-one counties on meeting the minimum federal requirement, her program was in arrears. My report to the person in charge, Ireta, was unequivocal: only 10 food-stamp families had been taught in 2004, shockingly well below the average count of 246 families. In my field audit report I noted that she'd spent her funds, over forty thousand dollars. As required, I asked for an explanation, copied Raymond and Beverly, and then forwarded the findings to the USDA. For confidentiality purposes, I left out the identity of all guilty parties and recommended that the manager be given another four months to comply. I reported to Ireta the result, and her response appeared to be both gracious and grateful.

Thinking about her petition to remove me as director, I wondered if she'd been nursing a grudge over the years. *Was she angry because I was responsibly doing my job? Or because she was embarrassed at being caught?*

I finished sorting the investigative boxes and removed one labeled Beverly Benford. In my mind, I fantasized building a big bonfire and throwing the whole box into it. Filled with cards, photographs, thank you notes, and other mementos that I'd kept over our twelve-year relationship, this box reeked of hypocrisy.

What happened to Beverly? I picked up the photo of Beverly and me standing next to Chef Martin Yan. We were all smiling.

Had she been stealing the whole time? I put everything back into the box, wondering if or when I'd missed a clue or a red flag. *She wasn't who I thought she was.* For some reason, I wasn't ready to destroy the personal effects of our relationship, at least not yet.

Of course, thinking about all this was a waste of time. I had to shove the whole thing aside and get back to working on things that mattered. I wasn't able to repair the past and would probably never understand it. As Daniel Ellsberg had said, I needed to create a new life and start over.

I finished cataloging the contents of the eighty boxes of evidence, including my past life with Beverly, returned them to my guest room closet, and locked the door.

On Friday, January 25, I drove to Davis. I was planning on moving my already packed work boxes into my new office on the third floor. In addition, the application paperwork for human subjects renewal for the statewide program was about to expire. Without the approval, staff would have to stop teaching clients. I drafted the application for Interim Director Hollinger, who'd been appointed on January 14 but was only just getting started. It seemed the decent thing to do.

When I got to Davis I found I was locked out. The temporary manager, Glenda, had changed the locks.

I sat in my car and sent an email to the dean's office. I was told I needed to wait for an invitation to enter my old office. I sent Glenda an email and waited three hours before driving home.

Glenda didn't respond until Sunday. She offered me a thirty-minute time slot on Wednesday, July 30, to move my things.

Meanwhile, the outside accounting firm, Lester & Forbes, asked to meet with me in their temporary headquarters in the internal auditing services office. We set up the first interview for February 12.

On Wednesday, January 30, during lunch, I moved my boxes to my new office and stopped by to introduce myself to Hank. He was very friendly and thanked me warmly for my help in pushing through some crucial paperwork needed for the program to continue. That was the first and last time we spoke.

Every morning during that period I'd wake to a flashback of something Raymond had said, or some memory of my now defunct relationship with Beverly. I began to recycle the investigation over and over. I figured this was just a phase in the mental processing of the crime.

Trying to tune it out wasn't working. Nothing seemed to grab me with the same intensity.

Reading books and going to movies was difficult: I simply couldn't follow the plot of either. I saw the movie *The Reader* three times, not ever managing to completely understand.

I spent a majority of my time during February sorting documents. I reorganized the investigation boxes down to sixty, recycling old stuff, and separately packing up papers unrelated to the investigation and returning them to Davis.

I went through the details over and over again in my head. The replaying became monotonous and engrossing. I couldn't get free of it.

I was obsessed by the investigation

On Tuesday, February 12, 2008, I met with two Lester & Forbes auditors at UC Davis's internal auditing office. Mateo Mendez and Julie Kardos, sophisticated and smart accountants who'd been with the firm for many years, began the interview by asking general questions. I discussed my past role at the university and recounted the history of the program. I specifically discussed the people who'd supervised Beverly, pointing out that I hadn't hired her.

I summarized the evidence I'd collected starting March 2, 2006, when I confronted Beverly in front of Raymond and culminating on August 28, 2006, when Beverly was put on investigatory leave. Glenda joined us in the interview room but didn't say a word the entire time. I got the feeling that she was there to keep tabs on me, but her presence was never explained.

Answering the questions without thinking too much, I must have sounded as though I was still director. It was hard to shed the skin I'd worn for so many years. Glenda was writing everything down, and the sounds of her scribbling made me laugh.

At one point, as she was flipping pages to keep up, I turned to her and quipped, "Am I talking too fast?"

I watched her write that down in large letters on her yellow notepad. Clearly, she didn't have a sense of humor.

"We have a spreadsheet of expenses charged to the program from 2002 to 2007 that we'd like to review with you," Mateo said as he handed me the ten-page document.

"Sure," I said looking at it. "I'll need a magnifying glass," I joked as my eyes squinted to read the tiny ledgers.

Luckily I brought my reading glasses. We discussed in detail every item purchased. Julie kept track of my responses.

"Tell us how equipment was ordered for your program," Mateo asked.

"As you know, we worked with forty-one counties throughout California, each one providing unique teaching methods. Each year programs would provide a justification to order equipment, which would then be approved by the USDA. Beverly would purchase the equipment based on the orders and have it sent to Davis for inventory purposes. After she entered the equipment into the inventory record, she'd ship it to the program. Beverly explained that this rather cumbersome process was to keep tabs of all equipment purchased," I said matter-of-factly. "She even maintained a list of inventory numbers. No one questioned her procedure. She gave me reports that were remarkably consistent with policy and since no one complained or challenged her, everything appeared to be in order."

I continued, "Beverly appeared to be very cautious and conservative about spending the program funds. She would question everything and everyone. No one complained about her to me, although I did know that many thought she was harsh and strict, which wasn't necessarily a bad thing for a manager."

As I answered questions on each item listed on the spreadsheet, I also provided details.

"This spreadsheet indicates two digital cameras were purchased for Madera County in 2005. The person who manages that program requested one. I didn't approve these purchases," I said, then added, "I'm going to speculate now. I think this was all Beverly. I suspect that she ordered one for Madera County and one for herself."

In conclusion, I said, "She didn't include these 2005 purchases on the inventory list she gave me that year. I didn't find out about these purchases until March 9, 2006."

"Wow," Julie said as she typed. "You really have a very good memory for details."

"Oh, yes," I said confidently. "I'll even send you the copy of the email I received from Beverly about this particular purchase. Beverly sent the email to cover up her DVD camcorder purchase; that's how she exposed the fact that she'd approved equipment purchases without having the authority to do so." I added teasingly, "The date was Thursday, March 9th."

"Thursday? You recall that March 9 a year ago was a Thursday?" Julie repeated, stunned. She was so curious that she searched for a calendar on the Web, and announced that March 9 was indeed a Thursday.

"I'll send you the email when I get back to my office," I volunteered. I didn't tell them that March 9 was the day I'd spent arguing with Beverly and Raymond on the telephone, finishing up with a drive to Davis. A day I was actually trying to forget.

Interested in finding out more about whistleblowers, I stumbled on a book called *Whistleblowers: Broken Lives and Organizational Power* by C. Fred Alford.[12] I was hoping that my experience wasn't unusual and I could learn from others.

Dr. Alford, a professor of government at the University of Maryland, College Park, had done a study of a couple dozen or more whistleblowers living in the Washington DC area. His book was very well-written and scholarly.

I was interested in understanding the whistleblower experience. I needed to come to grips with a lingering question—why me? Why did other people, the ones who knew about the crime, allow Beverly and Raymond to milk the university?

As I searched the book to answer my questions, I found many validating whistleblower stories. My belief in a just and honest world wasn't unique. Nor were any of the whistleblowers naïve, different, abnormal, crazy, or, as departmental chair Fred Stone claimed, out of step with the rest of the world.

My favorite parts in the book were the quotes from whistleblowers. One in particular nailed my own experience.

> And those "friends" you made, or thought
> you made, at work over the years, during
> countless team projects, holiday parties, office
> birthdays, etc.? People you've laughed with,
> shared photos of your kids, and . . . maybe even
> traveled with . . . ? The people . . . you spent
> more time with . . . Now, Whistleblower, you
> find you might as well have painted yourself
> green, stood on top of your desk, and shouted
> to your workmates that you're a . . . Martian.
> Some will look away in embarrassment. Oth-
> ers will tell you to stop complaining and get
> back to "work." And still others will elbow
> your peers in a knowing sort of way and aver
> that they always knew that there was some-
> thing just a tad touched about you . . . It is not
> just a matter of losing one's job but one's place
> in the world . . . It just makes the Whistle-
> blower more fearful.

In the beginning of March I heard that Glenda handed lay-off notices to all my former staff except Ginny. Ginny said that Rebecca took it very hard and left the office abruptly. Ryan wasn't surprised by the news and maintained his sense of humor to get him through that rough day.

I was shocked. I felt bad for Ryan and Rebecca, but there was nothing I could do.

"Was there any clue? Was this expected?" I asked Ginny.

"Nope. Glenda followed policy by the book. This notice was the warning," Ginny whispered.

"But what did Hank say?" I asked. "Did he explain why they got the boot?"

"Hank wasn't there!" Ginny told me. "There was a lady from human resources to make sure it was done properly." Ginny's voice lowered. "I have the feeling Glenda's hiring new people to do different kinds of work," she finished barely audible.

"But still," I protested, "she could have given them more than thirty days!"

"I feel bad that they're leaving and I'm not," Ginny said sounding guilty. "Don't get me wrong, I'm relieved that I was spared," she added. "I need this job. But who's going to do all the work?" she wondered.

I knew exactly how Ginny felt. We'd all been kicked in the pants, one way or another.

By April, interview requests by Lester & Forbes slowed. I packed up all my boxes again and put them back into the locked closet in the guest room. Now that my role in the investigation was winding down, it was time to officially move on.

But planning for my new role at the university, even contemplating it, proved difficult. I'd spent so many years conducting nutrition fieldwork to improve the health of low-income families, I wondered if I would be satisfied with studying poverty instead of trying to alleviate its worst effects? My work in the trenches helping families out of poverty was advocacy, not the stuff of academia. Normally, after twenty-five years at the university, I'd be coasting on my laurels, writing papers, giving talks, not creating a new existence. Even more unsettling, my only specific university assignment was to lay low.

The four-month "no fault" paid leave was to prepare for my return to the university as a faculty member doing research and teaching. Although my leave wasn't a sabbatical, I needed to invest my time in doing something interesting to *me*. This was indeed an opportunity to get my feet wet again.

The hardest part was accepting that my colleagues could be so cruel and that my relationships with many were over. I didn't want to spend the rest of my university life looking over my shoulder, but finding new faces in the academic world wasn't going to be easy.

Finally, after contemplating, reading, and studying new areas of focus, I was invited to give a public lecture on food stamps at Stanford University. A group called STOP Poverty sent me an email on April 15 asking if I was available on May 5.

I readily agreed. At Stanford, I could mix with faculty and students without the fear associated with my whistleblowing history. I thought this would be an opportunity to move in a new direction.

"I want to thank STOP Poverty for inviting me to speak today," I said relaxed and smiling, standing behind the podium after being introduced.

Following one of Stanford's medical doctors who'd spoken about his classy work on the economic effects of poverty, we'd just returned from a short break.

I looked around the room. They were all so young, the same age as my daughter, who was now a freshman.

I paused briefly to let those standing find a seat.

"I am speaking today about a topic very close to my heart." I moved my hand to my heart and noted that my pulse was rapid.

"I've been asked to talk about the Food Stamp Program," I continued. "I want to applaud the work of the STOP Poverty group that invited me to speak.

"I want to focus now on the health disparities of the poor." I was eager to share my two decades of experiences in the field on a number of chronic conditions. "Motivating people to be healthy must include providing knowledge and practical ideas about healthy food choices," I began. I handed out my paper on the link between eating a healthy diet and risk reduction of several chronic conditions, including Type 2 diabetes, hypertension, heart disease, stroke, some forms of cancer, and foodborne illness.

After discussing my paper on how nutrition education can lower the risk of many chronic conditions, I moved to a more hands-on discussion.

Using stories from my experiences as director, I felt the familiar pang of satisfaction. These young kids were interested in knowing how to help the most vulnerable populations. Discussing the food habits of poor families, I tried to prompt the students to think out loud.

"I have a question," one young woman asked. "How can poor families afford to eat a healthy diet?"

"Very good question," I answered. "You're correct that poor families have a harder time, especially now that food prices are at a record high. But, there are some practical tips on saving money and eating a healthy diet.

"For one, buying meat and poultry on sale and then using these protein sources in stews, soups, chili, and other dishes that stretch the food dollar can save money.

"For another, a vegetarian diet is less expensive," I suggested. I noted that many students were nodding and smiling.

"It also helps to understand the psychology of the grocery store set-up. Stores are stocked to get consumers to buy a lot of unnecessary items and most of these are the unhealthy choices.

"Where do you think the healthiest foods are found in a store?" I asked the group. Several of the students looked stumped.

"Next time you're shopping make a mental note where the fruits, veggies, milk products, breads, cereals, and protein sources like meats, poultry, eggs, fish are located in the store. You'll probably discover that you'll be cruising the entire store to find them," I explained.

"Placing all the basic dietary essentials at the back and sides of the store creates impulse buying of unnecessary and unhealthy foods," I pointed out.

"This is why shopping with a list saves money," I said. "A list will reduce temptation and gets you out of the store faster.

"Even better," I emphasized, "try this exercise. Go to the supermarket right after you gulped down a big meal. You'll stick to your list and nothing will tempt you, not even those chocolate-smothered graham crackers at the check-out stand that we can all live without."

This led to a discussion about the cost of a nutritious diet and how to save money shopping wisely.

"Here's another tip. The most expensive items are placed at eye level," I revealed. "Supermarket consultants have studied the behavior of the average consumer and have found that people buy items from the middle shelves. Customers are reluctant to bend down or jump up to compare prices," I said, smiling at the thought of shoppers jumping in the aisles. "But that's where you're going to find the healthy products," I said, glancing at the clock.

At the end, I briefly discussed my research on improved nutrition in families who prepare foods from scratch compared to those who buy already prepared foods.

"Your grandmother was right," I said in conclusion. "Cooking is essential to good nutrition. Foods prepared from scratch will taste better, be healthier, and in the long run, save money."

The sound of applause that in the past I'd taken for granted was suddenly uplifting and gratifying.

"I enjoyed talking with you. Thanks for inviting me, and let me know how I can help you in your work on stopping poverty."

After my talk a group of students came up and surrounded me. I met four or five who wanted to discuss the idea of starting a farmer's market in East Palo Alto.

As I drove home that evening I realized that I'd forgotten about the embezzlement during the whole day at Stanford. This was positive; I was moving on.

A few days later, I drove up to Davis. I'd been told to stay away from the department, so I went in the late afternoon to avoid bumping into anyone. The investigation was still ongoing, and Matt had told me that colleagues were feeling the heat. Another faculty member had her computer seized. Others were being scrutinized right and left from other funding agencies probably concerned that their funds might be misused.

Early in June, Leonard called. He sounded upbeat, hinting that he wanted to share some news about his book. Agreeing to meet again at Fat Apples, I swung by his Berkeley apartment to give him a lift.

In the car he was nervous; in fact, he didn't look good. When we got to Fat Apples, he confessed that the book on transformation he'd been working on for several years wasn't finished. He was agitated, something I'd never seen before.

"Do you want me to read it and give you comments?" I asked wondering why he asked to see me.

"Thanks, but no thanks," he said gruffly. "This isn't a social visit," he explained after ordering soup and a whole wheat roll.

I could tell that he was going to drop a bomb on me, and I wondered why I hadn't considered this when he called.

"I need money," he announced.

Determined not to get upset, I sat there and listened. I was paying for the house, Judith's education and her living expenses, and I didn't have any extra. I wasn't going to cave to his demands.

"What about your book? When will it be done?" I asked calmly trying to sound optimistic.

"I've missed the deadline," he confessed.

"Well, then call the publisher, explain your difficulty—what is it—writer's block—and renegotiate the deadline," I replied.

"I did that a year ago," he told me looking irritated.

"And what happened then?" I asked perplexed.

"Well, there is a problem with the advance," he added.

This was interesting to hear, as he had previously avoided acknowledging that there was one. "How much was the advance?" I asked.

"That's not relevant," he said stiffly.

"Is your publisher in the Bay Area?" I asked, wondering who

on earth would have given him an advance.

"Ah...well, this isn't a publisher issue," he stumbled, trying to avoid the question. He went on about something to do with an Internet piece he'd posted and how he'd gotten so many comments that he was still trying to sort out his own thinking. He rambled on about the book getting bigger, having difficulty integrating the components, and finally starting over.

"I've changed my view on the subject," he offered. "This has changed the book's timeline," he said, then struggled with the next sentence. ". . . not too happy that I'd spent the money," he finished. There was definitely something fishy with the story.

"This is the book on transformation, right?" I asked trying to recall the actual title.

"Yes," he said.

I stopped at this point, not wanting to make things worse. I was perplexed that anyone had gambled on this book or even on Leonard ever finishing it. He was good with the ideas part but poor on the execution. I returned to his book advance concern.

"You seem to be in a state of panic. It must be your worry about finishing the book. Maybe I could give you some help," I suggested.

"I don't need help with the book. I need cash," he asserted.

The rest of the meal we ate in silence.

I took him back to his Berkeley apartment and drove home. I found Leonard's book posted on the Web asking for comments. Called "Quaker Think Tank" the Web site referred people to my address and telephone number! Leonard had left years ago— why was he still using my address and telephone number?

He had posted several chapters. Called *The Transformation of Society*, it had an interesting premise.

> Individual and Societal Transformation:
> The Connection
> There is a legitimate concern for the need
> for a transformative change in the way we live.
> Some see it as essential if we are to prevent an

> irreversible degradation of the environment
> and increasing social strife . . . This . . . pro-
> poses a way to understand how societal trans-
> formation might come about . . .

Interesting. This was the part of Leonard that I admired. Then later on, the ideas began to unravel; oh dear, I said to myself, Leonard's book deal wasn't going to be a money-making proposition.

Leonard was probably running out of money. Now was the time to cut the cord before things really ran amok.

On June 10, Beverly pleaded guilty in federal court. The news was reported by Denny Walsh of the *Sacramento Bee* the next morning:

> Ex-UCD Employee Pleads Guilty to Theft
> A former University of California, Davis,
> employee pleaded guilty Tuesday in federal
> court to theft of government property . . . .Bev-
> erly Benford of Sacramento admitted a six-year
> spree of spending federal funds on hundreds of
> items for herself, including iPods, camcorders,
> digital cameras, home security systems, televi-
> sions and stereos . . . She admitted misiden-
> tifying purchases to make it appear they were
> appropriate expenditures. In other instances,
> she lied about where items had been delivered
> to conceal her theft.

I called Ginny to share the news.

"Ginny," I began, "it's Amy. Beverly pleaded guilty," I said rushing to tell her.

"She pleaded guilty," Ginny repeated all agog. "That's amazing! I never thought that would happen!"

After a pause, Ginny asked worried, "Did she get a plea

bargain?"

"I don't know," I answered. "We'll have to wait until her sentencing hearing to know what really happened."

We were happy to hear this news, although we wondered if somehow she'd escape punishment by a plea bargain.

The next day I drove up to Davis to meet with Dean Fitzpatrick about my office in the department. He said that he was going to find me a new office far away from the Food, Health and Society Department. In the meantime, I should continue to do my academic work at home. I chose environmental approaches to improve health, wanting more than ever to set off on a new direction.

On June 13, the story was reported by the campus in their Dateline UC Davis:

> Former Employee Pleads Guilty
> A former UC Davis employee pleaded
> guilty ... Assistant U.S. Attorney Steven
> Lapham said Beverly Benford ... admitted in
> a plea agreement to using $160,000 of funds
> ... for her own purposes. U.S. District Judge
> Lawrence Karlton sent the case to the U.S.
> Probation Department for recommendations
> on sentencing; he scheduled the next hearing
> for October 7 ...

Now that Beverly accepted responsibility in court, I expected some sort of announcement to clear my reputation. I was told by Frank, the LDO, that it would take a while before I heard anything official from the university.

In July, I received an email from a former staff member, Sandra Gutierrez, inviting me to a retirement party for one of my colleagues. Although this colleague hadn't signed the petition to remove me and I really wanted to attend, I knew that Raymond would be there. I sent a card and a check for the group gift, and called Sandra to personally relay my regrets.

Sandra, a young nutrition professional when I met her in 1980, was the mother of five grown-up sons and a smart community organizer delivering education to the food stamp clients.

On the telephone, Sandra announced that after almost thirty years she was being laid off in September. I assumed it was Glenda, the layoff queen, but didn't press for the details. I asked if she wanted a letter of recommendation. Sandra's reply was enthusiastic.

"Hell, yes! That's so kind of you," she said, asking me how I was doing.

"I'm good," I answered telling her about the talk I gave at Stanford and avoiding any discussion about the continuing investigation.

I sent Sandra a letter of recommendation, and for several weeks we communicated via email and by telephone. I didn't tell her that I was keeping a low profile or that the investigation was ongoing. We had a long history together, and I appreciated her upbeat response to the layoff.

The subject of Beverly finally came up. Sandra admitted she was shocked when she heard the news about the embezzlement.

"Beverly had been friendly to me, and she was oh-so-loyal to you," Sandra told me. "I couldn't believe what happened!"

"Yep," I shrugged. "I'm still trying to come to grips with it myself," I admitted. "There was a side to Beverly, well, let's just say, it's still a tragedy for all of us, especially the university," I finished sadly.

"I did have one occasion where Beverly made me uncomfortable," Sandra confided. "She tried to hit me up for cash," Sandra explained. "But I didn't have any money," she added. "I was kinda shocked. Here she was driving me to a meeting in her brand-new Mercedes SUV and asking me, the person who makes the least amount of money at UC, to help her out!"

"Did she tell you why she needed money?" I asked, curious.

"Her utility bill," she said. "She even showed me the warning letter. She was crying. I've seen those warnings many times from our clients. I've also seen the tears. I've worked with so many clients telling them not to ignore bills. They have to respond. I even held the hands of many clients to phone the utility company and work out an arrangement," she said proudly.

Sandra said she gave Beverly the same advice, that she should tell them she needed more time to pay the bill. "I have no idea if she did it or not. However, I do know that after that she wasn't so friendly."

Early August, I called a divorce attorney, consulted with him over the telephone, and prepared a draft agreement to buy Leonard's share of the house.

I phoned Leonard and discussed the agreement. He still seemed wary, actually arguing against the idea and insisting that I sell the house. After much prompting on my part, he agreed to think about my offer.

It was an unpleasant telephone conversation. He wasn't really interested in negotiating, he just wanted money.

A few days later, I received a letter from Franklin Taylor-Starr, the Local Designated Official (LDO) for whistleblowers, which surprised and shocked me. The letter wasn't about clearing my name and reputation. Instead, I was officially notified of a new investigation.

Suddenly, I was the subject of an investigation and charged with a number of misconduct allegations. Although not an indictment, at least not yet, this was a serious matter that could end my career at the university. The news knocked me off my feet.

Accused of a whole range of wrongdoing from grant mismanagement to allowing criminal activity to occur, the letter conveyed a serious tone. It included four specific investigative issues, some strange, some vague. I was accused of "improper delegation of financial and administrative control," or in layman's terms, allowing Beverly to run rampant with the funds.

The second and most bizarre of the allegations was that I "instructed [Beverly] to forge her signature on university travel vouchers."

The third allegation of pre-signing forms wasn't completely surprising as I'd already disclosed my mistake to the auditors voluntarily. However, all I'd done was pre-sign a few purchase orders for office supplies. The allegation in this letter was much more serious: "improperly pre-signed purchase requisitions." A purchase requisition was for expensive equipment costing over $2,500. I hadn't done that.

The last allegation was more subjective, although the most serious and challenging to rebut. I was accused of failing to take necessary action after a USDA audit in 2003 and that my actions or lack of actions resulted in millions of dollars that the university would have to return to the food stamp program.

The letter implied that I could be fired from my university position as a faculty member. Recalling that I hadn't yet signed the dean's Memorandum of Understanding (MOU) made me even more vulnerable.

Any one of these policy concerns could lead to my being dismissed and punished. Even if the letter didn't point out that my future was on the line, I knew what was at stake.

From August 15 to September 15, I prepared my defense. I dug back into the boxes that I'd shelved and tried to forget. It was oddly therapeutic and liberating to tell my side of the story. Now free to share all the dirty details about my experience at the university, I was ready to roar.

The sixty boxes of evidence all neatly organized and locked in my guest room were now going to serve a new purpose. My repeated attempts at correcting problems were documented. The lack of official support for my efforts to correct improper procedures, my belligerent colleagues who refused to comply, and my box of confidential audits that I'd done over the years protecting the reputation of my peers could now be revealed. The UC motto "Let there be light!" became my mantra.

The nitty-gritty details would tell my story. If anything, I was consistent about rules and compulsive about following them. I had stacks of emails that I sent repeatedly to everyone, reminding them of federal requirements. I had responses from colleagues bellyaching that I was rigid and conservative. I documented my repeated efforts to follow policy and to police it. I even had emails from officials telling me to "back off," when I found problems. It wasn't a pretty picture, but I was anxious to paint it.

Now that the cat was out of the bag, I provided countless examples of problems that I'd kept confidential to protect the privacy of others.

One particular event in Northern California provided, I believed, a good example of my efforts to ward off criminal activity. A proposal to assist low-income schools provided a list of people working in the program. After phoning all the individuals on the list, I documented that these people weren't working, and denied this portion of the budget. Again, I didn't reveal the name of the individual responsible to the university officials, who applauded my efforts to maintain program integrity.

I managed to stay on speaking terms with this colleague, believing that I handled the situation fairly and discreetly. However, it was no surprise to me that her name was on the retaliation letter written by Ireta.

I prepared a six-page response with twenty exhibits of documentation, including eighteen emails, ten letters, six reports, seven meeting minutes, five federal regulation documents, seven audit reports, six federal forms with instructions, and one power-point presentation, all supporting my defense, covering years 2001 to 2007.

On Tuesday, September 16, I handed in my 300-page defense—a 6-page letter with 294 pages of exhibits—to the Davis official in charge of the review. I was satisfied that I'd done everything I could to show that I had followed university policy and did my job as best that I could under the limitations imposed by and the deception of my supervisor, the departmental chair.

It would be many months more before this investigation would be completed. Many high-level people, vice-chancellors and others who didn't know me from Adam, would be interviewed. My defense would consume the time and energy of a number of individuals.

The investigative process, now familiar to me, seemed fair and square. I believed that the university would handle my case with the due diligence it deserved. I'd put my best foot forward and hoped it would cross the finish line.

No longer afraid, remarkably free of scars, I believed my response was sufficient. My faith in myself was restored. The healing had finally begun.

On September 30, I'd received notification of a letter from Chancellor David Russell, someone I held in high esteem. I was asked to come to his office to pick it up.

I arrived at the chancellor's office and was given the letter. I opened it in my car. With my heart racing, I quickly read it and was riveted by the last paragraph:

> Dear Dr. Joy:
>
> I understand that certain steps have been taken to assure your transition to new responsibilities in a new environment. I am grateful to you for filing your report of improper governmental activities with the campus administration as it allowed the University to identify and correct a variety of significant problems . . . I also appreciate your continuing cooperation with and assistance to the campus administration as it continues.

I sat in my car as tears of joy moistened my face. It was a welcome relief that the chancellor recognized that I was motivated to do the right thing and that the university acknowledged in writing that corrections were needed.

Now the only remaining issue was whether or not I was going to be fired. The jury was still out on that volatile question.

In early October 2008, Leonard called and invited me to join him at a coffee shop across the street from his Berkeley apartment.

I arrived a little early and ordered a latte at the counter. While waiting for my latte, I heard Leonard's voice behind me, "Could you get me a cup of English Breakfast tea?"

He walked over to a table nearby and sat down.

I brought over his tea and my coffee and joined him. He wasn't his usual cheerful self.

"I want to talk to you about money," he uttered as I picked up my cup.

"Okay," I said waiting, sipping the very hot foamy top slowly.

"We need to get going on a financial settlement," he added stiffly. I noted he had a file in front of him.

"I agree," I stated. "Remember you were going to get back to me about my offer to purchase your share of the house," I said.

"Never mind about that," he said sounding irritated.

"I heard you received a reward for blowing the whistle," he announced aggressively.

"Blowing the whistle? Reward? Who told you that?" I asked, wondering how this gossip reached Leonard.

"You did," he said, picking up his cup of tea and glancing at me sideways.

"No, I didn't," I answered sarcastically. "I didn't tell you about a reward because there isn't a reward." I was seething. He acted very coy.

"You need to provide to me all your bank statements. I have the right to receive half the reward," he said, pounding his fist hard on the table. He snarled adding insult to injury.

"Leonard, I'm going to repeat myself. There isn't a reward. Who suggested to you that I received a reward?" I asked again.

He was completely silent.

"Let's meet with Bernard and discuss our financial settlement with him," I suggested hoping that Leonard still trusted our mutual friend Bernie, a successful and now retired corporation attorney.

"I'll set a date," he said eagerly, asking me for his telephone number.

Leonard gave me no clue as to whether or not he was going to agree to my idea of buying his share of the house. I wondered what he had up his sleeve.

Judith came home for the Thanksgiving weekend. On Wednesday before Thanksgiving, I drove her over to visit Leonard. When we arrived at his Berkeley flat, Judith called him on her cell phone to let him know she arrived. He asked to speak to me.

"I need money. You have to sell the house," he announced, raising his voice.

"Don't be ridiculous," I answered. "I'm not selling the house."

"Well then you need to give me my share—$500,000!"

"Our house isn't worth $1 million and even if it were, the amount of money we'd get would be much lower than it is worth. We still have a mortgage that would need to be paid off first," I stated, trying to sound logical and relaxed. Here we go again, I said to myself.

"Leonard, let's talk about this later. Judith wants to see you. We're right outside."

I gave Judith back her cell phone and told her to call me when she wanted to be picked up.

A couple of hours later, Judith arrived home. Leonard had borrowed a car from a friend and dropped her off. She handed me an envelope.

"Dad asked me to give this to you," she said and then went into her room to call a friend.

The letter was a threat, and not a subtle one. It had the appearance of looking like a lawyer had written it, with a bunch of "Whereas" at the beginning of every sentence. But the real purpose was to threaten me, and I doubted that a lawyer had written it. "...Amy shall have sixty days to decide whether she will purchase Leonard's interest in the Property. If she decides not to do so, the Property will be listed for sale."

I felt sick. Leonard's so-called interest in the Property was stated as a ridiculous half-a-million. Selling the house, the one I'd envisioned that we'd leave to Judith, at an all-time economic housing low was just plain stupid.

I arranged for us to meet with Bernie on November 29, 2007, and drafted an agreement for me to buy his share by getting a bank loan. I paid for an appraiser to value the house using both square footage and comparison prices of houses that had been sold in the area. The appraisal value was set at $760,000.

We met for an hour on Saturday, November 29. Leonard balked on the deal because he wanted more money, but in the end, he couldn't really argue the numbers. Taking the value of $760,000 and subtracting the 6 percent selling fee, the mortgage owed on the house, Leonard's share of supporting Judith, taxes, house insurance, and other expenses that I'd paid for him would leave $200,000. Splitting that in half, we'd each get $100,000. He looked over the house appraisal and what would be left. He signed the agreement on November 29, which was witnessed by Bernie, who pretty much stayed silent during the whole discussion.

Although I felt the agreement was reasonable, I wasn't sure if I could afford to pay it. I didn't disclose to Leonard, Bernie, or anyone else that I was a subject of an investigation and that my future employment at UC and thus my salary were uncertain.

On Monday, December 1, 2008, I asked the LDO when the investigation of the allegations against me would be completed. I was given the impression that it would still take a couple of months.

After all this, I told myself, *I'm not giving up. I love my job at the university.* I gambled that my future was secure and moved forward optimistically.

Leonard, after agreeing to co-sign the bank loan, reneged at closing and told me, not too politely and in no uncertain terms, to hand over ten thousand dollars if I wanted his signature on the final loan papers.

"No money, no signature," he snarled.

On Tuesday, December 9, I met Leonard at Bank of America. I deposited the ten thousand into his bank account. He seemed upbeat and happy. It was Judith's birthday, and she was having a final at UCLA, returning home on Wednesday. I'd managed to get her a cheap flight and wondered if Leonard had made arrangements to see her. I invited him to join us for a birthday dinner.

He was evasive about joining us, so I dropped the idea.

The next day Judith arrived at the Oakland Airport, and we drove home. She was excited about a class she'd taken in community health and said that this was what she wanted to study. I was pleased.

When I told her about my plan to celebrate her birthday and that I had invited Leonard, she told me he was returning to live in England!

When we arrived home, I called Leonard's apartment, and heard his girlfriend's voice on his answering machine. This startled me even more.

"You've reached the home of Tricia and Leonard. Please leave us a message."

Leonard returned to England. I took Judith out to celebrate her twentieth birthday without him. We dined at Rivoli's, a lovely restaurant in Berkeley owned by Roscoe and Wendy, a couple I'd chatted with over the years. Wendy, a magnificent chef, whipped up a special birthday dessert for Judith. While waiting, we talked about the future.

"Mom, I'm really looking forward to going to see Damon. Thank you for all your support," she said, her eyes sparkling.

Judith was about to leave to visit her steady beau, Damon.

"I'm so happy you found someone really special," I answered, hearing the rumblings of a happy birthday song inching toward our table. We both giggled as the dessert was placed in front of Judith.

Blowing out the glittering candles on top of a luscious homemade ice cream sundae, Judith closed her eyes to make a wish, most likely about Damon.

As I picked up my spoon to dig into the cascading heaps of hot fudge, I also made a wish.

May Judith's life be filled with joy, happiness, and most of all, an unshakable belief in herself.

On Monday, December 15, 2008, I called Matt to tell him that I was moving out of the Food, Health and Society Department. The dean's office had located a place for me in Environmental Horticulture. I noted that they found the place but hadn't yet given me a key.

I asked Matt if he'd seen Raymond.

"Nope," Matt said over the telephone. "He doesn't seem to be around these days."

"I wonder if he'll ever have to face the music of what he did," I asked, wondering if he knew anything.

"Do you believe in karma?" Matt answered.

"Yes," I answered. "Raymond damaged his own future. If I were in charge of EQUINOX, I'd question every dollar he'd ever spent," I finished.

"Well," Matt laughed, "you may be right about that. Looks like Raymond doesn't have his groupies anymore. They're all gone. Everyone's moved on. He's got a tiny, empty office; like a captain without a ship. Most likely he's out of money."

"No money?" I said crassly. "Poor Raymond . . . that's gotta hurt."

Raymond wasn't the only one without funds. In early January, Leonard began leaving messages on my answering machine asking for more money. He repeatedly said he was desperate for cash. He ranted and raved about putting the house on the market. It was as though he'd never signed the agreement. Worse, I wondered what had happened to the ten thousand!

I heard from several different sources that he was traveling throughout England with his girlfriend. I pictured them on a ten-grand spending spree.

I'd been concerned that Leonard would return to England,

the motherland of his first marriage. In a twinkling of an eye, I shifted into first gear. Now was the time to divorce, before he, poof! vanished into thin air.

I talked to a couple of attorneys and was given a heads-up on how much I'd have to pay. Divorcing in California, a no-fault, fifty-fifty community property state, wasn't going to be in my favor no matter which way the cake was sliced.

I'd hoped to negotiate with Leonard although I knew this was a shot in the dark. Clearly, Leonard wasn't going to let me buy his share of the house. He signed the agreement so I'd cough up the ten thousand. I believed his following through with the transfer of the property to me was iffy. And now with his escape to England, all bets were off.

On January 6, 2009, I called the auditors to find out what happened in federal court to Beverly Benford. Because she pleaded guilty in June, a jury trial wasn't required. The decision on her sentence would be determined by a federal judge. I wouldn't have to testify at her trial.

Joseph, one of the auditors, read me the university's press release.

"Beverly Benford was sentenced to one year and one day in federal prison and ordered to pay restitution of more than $128,000. Following her sentence, she was ordered to serve three years of probation."

I asked about the probation.

Joseph wasn't really sure about the ins and outs of the probation system. "After she serves time in federal prison," he said, "she'll have an additional three years to be a law-abiding citizen. She'd probably be hauled back to jail if she violates any law," he added. "Parolees have many restrictions."

He read the end of the press release.

"She was ordered to surrender herself to the marshals on February 17, 2009," Joseph concluded.

I called Ginny to share the news.

"Well, she's been sentenced to one year and one day in federal prison!" I told her trying to maintain my composure.

"Whoa." Ginny was shocked. "Is she going there today?"

"Well," I answered, "her sentence begins in mid-February."

"I bet she's goin' to be a no-show," Ginny worried out loud.

"Nope, not possible," I replied. "The federal marshals will escort her on February 17," I answered, picturing her being hauled away in handcuffs.

On January 6, 2009, *UC Davis News & Information* issued a press release:

> Former Staffer Goes to Prison
> A former UC Davis employee—who had earlier pleaded guilty to using $160,000 of funds from a federal program for her own purposes—was sentenced January 6 in Sacramento to serve 12 months plus one day in prison . . . and pay restitution of $128,681.
> U.S. District Judge Lawrence Karlton ordered Beverly Benford, who was in the courtroom, to surrender herself on Feb. 17 . . . to a U.S. marshal.
> Assistant U.S. Attorney Steven Lapham said the amount of restitution was determined by the total of the misappropriation funds less the value of items recovered.
> The alleged misappropriation of funds was initially reported to UC Davis officials in August 2006 as a whistleblower complaint.

The *Sacramento Bee* also reported the story on January 7:

> Ex-UCD Worker Gets Prison Term for Theft
> A former University of California, Davis, employee was sentenced Tuesday in federal court to a year and a day in prison . . . Beverly

> Benford . . . pleaded guilty in June, admitting
> a six-year spree of spending federal funds on
> hundreds of items for herself, including iPods,
> camcorders, digital cameras, home security
> systems, televisions and stereos . . . She admit-
> ted misidentifying purchases . . . lied about
> where items had been delivered to conceal her
> thievery . . .

The story was picked up by Associated Press and a number of stories appeared throughout California, including *SFGate. com*, *S.F. Examiner*, *Sacramento Business Journal*, *Daily Democrat -Woodland*, *Daily News-Red Bluff*, *Las Vegas Sun*, *L.A. Times*, and *Fresno Bee*.

That evening, Ginny called me at home. "Hey, Beverly going to prison was reported on KCRA-TV!" Ginny said very excited.

"I'd thought I wouldn't feel anything," I replied. "But I do. Justice was served and she's going to be held accountable for what she did. It's quite wonderful."

"So, now what?" asked Ginny.

"We celebrate!" I cheered breaking into song.

"*I feeeeeel good*," I rasped, mimicking soul singer James Brown.

"*Da, da, da, da, da, da, daaaaa*," rocked Ginny.

"*I knew that I would, now*," I crooned.

"*So gooood! So gooood! I got yooou! Ahh, ahh, ahhh, ahhaaa.*"[13]

9 | We Are the Champions!

Beverly entered the Federal Correctional Institute for Women on February 17, 2009, to begin her one year plus one day sentence. Using the "Inmate Locator" on the Web, I confirmed her arrival at the Dublin facility, the only federal prison for female inmates in California.

I pulled out the box of mementos of my life with Beverly and took it upstairs to my living room to sort it out along with my feelings. A year had passed since I'd locked up the sixty boxes of evidence in the closet of my guest room of my home. Feeling a desire for closure, I was ready to face the truth.

This "Beverly" box contained a slew of reminders of our relationship. Three years ago, March 2006, I'd put the relationship on hold when I caught Beverly stealing. Having thrown everything that Beverly ever gave me into this box, I'd been waiting a long time for this moment. I wanted concrete answers. Why did she steal? Why did she deceive me?

Looking back, I recalled when Raymond insisted on giving Beverly another chance. I went along with his idea, hoping for some sort of redemption. Little did I know his true motivation.

The investigation revealed both Raymond and Beverly's intention. Beverly had been embezzling for years, and Raymond was covering it up. Both were deceiving me.

Sitting on the couch next to the box, I opened it to look at the many cards, letters, and photos from Beverly. The card on top was one I'd read many times.

On the envelope, "Amy" was handwritten in Beverly's soft

swirls. A hand-painted sea shell glistened on the cream cover of the card. This magnificent shell sparkled with an iridescent mother-of-pearl cone weaving zigzag lines of silver. Beverly had seen my shell collection grow over the years with shells from beaches in California, Greece, New York, Italy, Australia, and even England. All my excursions were memorialized with a shell displayed prominently on my desk.

This was one classy card, carefully selected to convey an intimacy that squared with her handwritten message inside. I opened the card to read what Beverly had written.

Dear Amy,

I looked back at the years we shared are the absolute best times. We think the same. You are my "best friend." You know that I'm here for you through thick and thin. You are the greatest friend I ever had!
I am so touched by you. I know your heart. I will never change and always be your friend. You have to know when others fail you, I'm always there for you.
I love you a lot because of who you are. No one will come between us. We are a two-some in one mind.

Love, Beverly

It was dated September 18, 2005. I vividly recalled Beverly giving it to me. I was touched by her emotional vulnerability and friendship. But now, all I could see was the naked truth, her real purpose. It was her veiled attempt to distract me from what was really going on. September 18, 2005 was ten days after Tessa reported Beverly's travel fraud to Raymond, resulting in Tessa's resignation. I was attending our Food Stamp national conference in Washington DC and became alarmed when Beverly didn't show up at the meeting on Sunday, September 11.

It would take another six months before I found evidence of embezzlement. Beverly and Raymond must have panicked when they thought their gig was up and were desperately trying to cover their tracks.

Demanding that I keep away from Beverly right after my return from DC, Raymond created a handy ploy to keep me in the dark. And Beverly did what she thought would be effective—her false intimacy. She gave me this card then continued to embezzle all the way to her last day of work a year later!

Putting the card aside, I closed the box of mementos; I'd seen enough. The real message was pretty clear: Beverly had played me, big time. Raymond had, too.

I wanted to be a compassionate friend in the same way I wanted to help the poor, the needy, and the disenfranchised members of society. In all my attempts to go to bat for Beverly, I couldn't see that she wasn't either a needy comrade or a fallen idol; she was a crook.

I let go of the hurt. No longer controlled by the need to forgive Beverly and all the other people who'd let me down over the years, I walked outside to my recycling bin, opened the box, and unceremoniously tossed in the rest of the mementos. *Good-bye Beverly.*

I kept just the shell card to take back to Davis. *I'll hang on to this one,* I told myself feeling stronger. *This will remind me of a valuable life lesson that I've finally learned.*

Washing my hands in the kitchen sink, the ancient memory of a past trauma returned. The child abandoned on the beach, clinging to the rock and waiting to be rescued, swirled gently through my mind. This time the image didn't grab hold of me as it had in the past. I wasn't afraid anymore. I let go of the grief that had held me captive all these years.

It was time to get off the rock.

On March 7, 2009, I received an email from the provost's office that a letter was ready for me to pick up. On March 10, I

drove to Davis and waited in the chancellor's office receptionist area. Assistant Vice-Provost Eloise Summers invited me to
use her office to read the four-page letter and seventeen-page
investigative report. The letter sent by Vice-Provost Regina
Elizabeth Lawry, known for her wisdom, honesty, and integrity,
reported the findings on the investigation against me. Titled
"Report of Investigation—Allegations of Grant Mismanagement" the letter went on to specify the findings of the investi-
gations.

> The allegation that you improperly pre-
> signed [forms] . . . is substantiated. This
> happened once in calendar year 2000. The
> findings, however, note potential mitigating
> circumstances. You self-reported the incident
> to Internal Auditing Services . . . you followed
> up on the use of the pre-signed documents . . .
> nothing improper resulted . . . no discipline is
> warranted.
>
> • The allegation concerning improper dele-
> gations of financial and administrative controls
> was not substantiated . . .
>
> • The allegation that you instructed [Beverly
> Benford] to forge her signature . . . is not sub-
> stantiated.
>
> • The allegation that you improperly failed
> to take corrective action in response to the
> findings of a 2002-03 USDA review is not
> substantiated.
>
> There is no evidence to suggest that you
> engaged in any kind of intentional misconduct
> . . . Nevertheless, you were the person ulti-
> mately in charge of the $13 million grant that
> has been seriously and criminally mishandled
> . . . The University has been publicly embar-
> rassed and its stewardship of these government
> monies has been openly called into question. . .

At the same time, I appreciate the courage and conviction that you demonstrated in bringing to light your grave concerns about the situation and disclosing critical information to the university. Your unselfish actions allowed the university to identify and address the grant administrative problems and helped prevent future problems. I understand that [Dean Fitzpatrick] has continued to work with you to provide institutional support necessary to regenerate your research efforts and move forward . . . I would like to extend my best wishes for success as you move in this direction.

Sincerely,
Vice-Provost Regina Elizabeth Lawry

A seventeen-page investigative report provided details on all the charges against me. On the charge of unsatisfactory performance by a principal investigator (PI), the report stated that

Block Joy has not demonstrated unsatisfactory work performance as the PI . . . come to this conclusion primarily because . . .Block Joy was being actively deceived by [Beverly Benford] . . . Block Joy labored under difficult circumstances in which the former department chair [Raymond Savage] marginalized her . . . disregarded Block Joy's leadership . . . as PI.

By all indications . . . Block Joy served in the capacity of . . . PI . . . for many years without incident or complaint from her administrators, CDSS [food stamp agency], or the USDA. In one instance where . . . Block Joy was confronted by a situation that arguably best fits

the definition of the work "duty," one con-
cludes she acted appropriately, even admirably
. . . she turned into a whistleblower and raised
her suspicions with the university, unleashing a
chain of events that have been extremely difficult for her both personally and professionally.

Other charges were discussed in detail, including that I placed
too much trust in an employee, failed to set up fraud controls,
and exhibited negligence and incompetence. All charges were
dismissed. The letter and report officially cleared me of all allegations, providing the final resolution that I'd hoped for.

Assistant Vice-Provost Summers returned to her office, quietly shut the door, and sat down behind her desk. She didn't
say anything, although I guessed there was a lot she wanted to
say but couldn't. I sang out, "Yippee!", grinning earnestly. She
nodded, her eyes dancing in response. The feeling of liberation
was exquisite.

"I'm free!" I declared, radiating joy.

The evening of May 6 I received a call from Stuart, my
brother. Our father had a fall and was in Kaiser Hospital, Walnut Creek. I called Dad and we chatted on the telephone.

"I'm fine," he said in good spirits. "I'm going home tomorrow," he told me.

My father was living in Walnut Creek with his second wife.
He had retired from the Nuclear Regulatory Commission in
Washington and moved to California in 1985, five years after
my mother died. I'd seen him frequently and called weekly to
chat. The past few years he'd suffered some memory loss and
had become housebound. He did have one favorite pastime—
playing bridge. He was an accomplished player and instruc-
tor, and played rain or shine, every week at the Walnut Creek
Senior Center.

Thursday after work, I went to visit him in the hospital.

"Hi Dad," I said when I walked into his room. "It's Amy."

He brightened, and said softly, "Hi Amy. How nice of you to visit me!" I was enchanted by his lively spirit and happiness to see me.

"How are you feeling?" I asked. He looked pretty good, although the heart monitor indicated that his heartbeat was rapid.

The doctor told me they were going to sedate him to slow down his heart and expected to release him by the weekend. They thought he probably had a minor heart attack, which caused his fall. He hadn't broken anything, and they were waiting on the enzyme tests to determine the extent of heart damage. He wasn't in pain and was very keen to get home.

A couple days later I returned to his hospital room, bringing some music to cheer him up. I was told that he had a good night and his condition had steadied. My father loved Frank Sinatra. I showed him the tape and my player. He smiled.

"I'm going to play your favorite Sinatra song," I said.

As I put the Sinatra tape into my cassette player, I recalled a funny story. Sometime in 1957 my father made a 45 recording of one of Sinatra's hits for my mother, Ruthie. It was 1960 when Mom sold it at her garage sale for a dime to a family friend. The daughter of my mother's friend, Ellie, found it four years later, invited me over, played the record, and quizzed me on the singer's identity. I had no idea that my father had made a recording until I saw the label: "For Ruthie, Love Sy." I gave Ellie a dime and ran home to return it to Dad.

The Sinatra tape began playing.

"I've got you under my skin," crooned ol' blue eyes. [14]

Dad brightened and I saw a flash of recognition in his eyes. I took his hand and spoke to him softly.

"Dad, this was the song you made for Mom," I said, showing him the picture of Sinatra on the tape. "Do you remember?" As I held my father's hand, stoking it, we sang softly together.

"Don't you know you fool, you never can win
Use your mentality, wake up to reality . . ."

I gazed fondly at my father as the song ended. He seemed to be deep in thought. I wondered what memories the music brought back. Was it the spell that my mother had cast over him that snared him right from the start? I was quite aware of those feelings. I, too, had been snared.

I talked to my father as the tape continued to play other Sinatra favorites. We reminisced about the good times. Like the secret return of his record, I'd never shared with him that I was a whistleblower.

As we chatted a little and he drifted off to sleep, I recalled some secrets that I never really understood, especially the ones related to my father's work on the Manhattan Project and his secret mission to Nagasaki after the bomb dropped. My father kept his lifelong promise and never revealed what he knew.

Later that day, just after the nurses gave my father his lunch, he had a second heart attack, which was much more serious. I was in the room when it happened. He said he didn't feel any pain, although I could see by the expression on his face that something had happened.

He was clutching his stomach and I called his doctor who administered heart medication, a beta-blocker to slow the heart rate, which was now out of control. The medication worked fast and he became peaceful again. Because of his age, eighty-nine, and his frail condition, surgery to repair the blockage wasn't a possibility. Still the doctor gave him a good chance of recovery.

I called my brother who was living in Spokane, Washington, and he flew down to see Dad, arriving on Mother's Day 2009. I picked him up at the airport and tried to prepare him. I called Judith to let her know about the second heart attack. That afternoon when my father became lucid, we all said good-bye.

He went to sleep and died peacefully at six o'clock in the afternoon. My father had led a very long and healthy life, and I was comforted by the thought that he hadn't suffered.

My grieving for my eighty-nine-year-old father was different than it had been for my mother. My mother died at fifty-three in 1980 in Washington DC. She had lung cancer and over the prolonged course of her illness, I tried to practice saying good-bye. When she finally died, I was grief stricken. I returned home to California to start my new job at the University of California on April Fools' Day the same year. Ironically, that same week, I bumped into my future husband at the Zellerbach Hall box office. He was without cash and soon after buying him the concert seat next to mine, I fell madly in love. Did I fill the painful emptiness of grief with the excitement of romance? Was that how I recovered from the loss of my mother?

With my father, things were different. It felt sudden and unexpected. I wasn't ready to comprehend that he'd passed on, and I clung to memories of him. The last conversation I had with my father on the telephone just before his fall became a poignant reminder of our relationship.

My father had played bridge as usual the Friday before he fell. I'd spoken to him on Saturday, and he'd told me the same happy story I'd heard and enjoyed many times before.

"Amy, you'll never believe what happened yesterday! It's amazing. We won the bridge championship! We won! We won!" my father reported joyously on the phone.

"You're the champ!" I answered enthusiastically.

It'd been a few years since he and his bridge partner actually won that bridge championship, but in his mind it was only yesterday.

After my father died, Leonard, now residing in England, continued to badger me, leaving disturbing messages on my message machine and threatening me.

I didn't trust him. If I'd learned anything at all, it was that some people just don't play fair.

I decided to move forward on the divorce and called an attorney that a friend recommended.

Her paralegal, Leslie, answered the phone. She collected information on our names, birth dates and places, my address and telephone number.

"When did you get married?" Leslie asked me.

"July 20, 1986."

"Are you legally separated?"

"Oh no," I said cautiously. "And my husband is still covered by my health insurance through work. We are living apart," I answered feeling a little nervous, not wanting to rock the boat about his health insurance.

"Any children?"

"Our daughter Judith is twenty years old now," I answered aware that there wouldn't be any issues related to child custody since Judith was over eighteen.

"Is your husband providing you any spousal support?" she asked.

"No, it's the other way around," I said. "I provide money to him, or I did," I said, recalling the ten thousand dollars that I'd transferred to his account only five months ago. In fact, I'd paid for everything—mortgage, taxes, insurance, and Judith's educational expenses.

"What date did your marriage end?"

"A date...." I stammered. "That's a good question...the end of a marriage." In my mind I pictured myself throwing Leonard's clothes out the window and yelling down at him—*It's over!*

After we hung up, I thought a lot about the ups and downs of our marriage. A few days later I received Leslie's list of documents needed for the divorce. Besides deeds, purchase information on our house, copies of the title, loan documents, property taxes, credit card and bank statements, there was a table to provide an estimation of everything that was spent the month prior to separation.

I went downstairs to the office where I kept all the house stuff. Neatly labeled "House Documents," I began to sort through all the papers that I'd saved over the years. I found everything I needed—titles, deeds, loan docs from various banks that bought and sold our mortgage starting in 1990. I had credit card statements, bank accounts and my tax returns dating back to 1980.

I recalled the counseling session that Leonard had arranged. Suddenly I was transported back to our therapy session where he provided all the gory details.

"I'm here to raise a subject that will be difficult for Amy," Leonard told the therapist not even looking at me.

"I don't have any hope for a relationship with Amy," he continued, "and I'm leaving. If I am to value myself, I need to tell Amy that I'm separating. I'm moving out," I recalled Leonard saying in his thick British accent.

Stunned on that sunny day, I believed he was being overly dramatic until I saw the "DissoMaster" and how much alimony I would be required to pay. I couldn't recall if the young therapist uttered a word the entire fifty-minute session.

Now, sitting at the kitchen table, I considered all the dusty memories. Why did I stay, I wondered, and why hadn't we officially divorced? The answer, although complex, was painful. Now I wasn't so sure that this was strictly a money decision. Was I really just waiting for Leonard to become self-sufficient? I believed the real issue was a need to take control of my own destiny.

Of course there was also the issue about the house. I'd known for a long time that a divorce would require me to sell it.

There's no place like home, I said to myself, now a decade wiser. I peered out my kitchen window. Two squirrels darted up and down a majestic redwood tree, romping together playfully.

Leslie's question was answerable. Our marriage had an ending date that Leonard couldn't object to—January 19, 2001. Even though it was now 2009, our marriage had ended long ago.

I put together my responses and called Leslie back. We discussed the costs of divorce which included her boss's hourly fee of $425 plus a couple of thousand dollars to serve Leonard in England and pay for the court costs. I asked Leslie for referrals to less expensive lawyers.

No longer traumatized as I had been when Leonard announced the end of our marriage, my feelings had changed. I was stronger.

I called one of the referrals. Mr. David Powers was straightforward and courteous. Answering his questions, I knew exactly what I wanted. I was ready to take the plunge.

In order to comply with the financial aspects of the divorce, I would sell the house. Making no bones about it, losing my

home was something I had avoided. I loved the house with its
Zen-like setting of redwood trees and creek. But now, I was
ready to leave the nest.

I sent my responses for the divorce declaration as the peti-
tioner. Leonard would be served the moment he set foot on
American soil. Keeping this under wraps, I told no one.

Leonard would get the money he'd been hounding me for. I'd
fought the good fight long enough. It was time to go for broke!
I wanted the prize I'd coveted for years—my independence and
freedom.

In the middle of May, Dean Fitzpatrick sent me my Memorandum of Understanding—the unsigned MOU about my
future work at the university for review, revision, and my signature. Reading the original MOU I'd drafted almost eighteen
months before, I was surprised how much had changed.

I updated my job description and my office location. My
new position, office, and faculty appointment were now in the
dean's office. My salary reduction concern from 2007 was also
resolved. I was currently being considered for a promotion
which I anticipated would be approved and would ultimately
increase my salary.

I revised the MOU and returned it to Dean Fitzpatrick for
his review. I was going to now report to the executive dean
under Dean Fitzpatrick. My new department was the dean's
office at 150 Mrak Hall.

A few days later, Dean Fitzpatrick accepted all my revisions.

I was pleased by the university's show of support. My new
office in Environmental Horticulture was serene and peaceful,
and located near the arboretum, far from the department where
Raymond had once ruled.

Since my new position would be in the College of Agricultural and Environmental Sciences (CA&ES), I spiffed up my
job description to be in sync with my new home. My area of
work became Nutritional Ecology, a field based on examining
relationships between health, food acquisition, and sustainabil-

ity. This broad field was trendy and consistent with my interests in nutrition, health policy, and the environment. I developed a proposal for a new class that I wanted to introduce to students at UC Davis. I called it: "Eating Green."

On June 9, I went up to Davis to get a tour of my new office. I was pleased with the historic brown-shingled cabin office. Built in 1922, the sturdy bungalow was part of the original horticulture complex located near the true geographic center of the Davis campus. One of the earliest wood-shingled structures on the campus when Davis was the University Farm School that Peter Shields had championed in 1905, it was surrounded by trees, with a greenhouse next door and a path to the Arboretum Waterway, a public garden with over four thousand kinds of trees and plants stretching for over one hundred acres. The dean's office was going to have it cleaned and furnished before handing over my key. I'd planned to meet Ginny for a coffee before leaving Davis that day. I called her when I arrived in her department parking lot, and she invited me into the office to meet with the recently hired director, Trent Richardson.

I'd known Trent for years and had worked with him when he was at the California Department of Social Services doing exactly what I was doing at UC. Trent was an experienced and savvy administrator. We'd worked together on a number of food stamp projects. I was pleased that he was hired as the new director. I'd heard that the national search identified a number of qualified professionals, many were interviewed, and Trent was selected.

"Our director wants to see you," Ginny raved with gusto. "He's been asking me when you'd stop by," she told me over the telephone.

I walked into the office and Ginny rushed over to hug me.

"Hey," she said when she saw me. "You've cut your hair! You look so jazzy with your bouncy ringlets." She smiled, her eyes sparkling. It was great to see Ginny again.

"I'm incognito," I joked.

My long hair was styled to be shoulder length and had become very curly, as it was when I was younger. Wearing casual clothes and sunglasses, my non-director appearance was meant to match my desire for simplicity.

Ginny introduced me to the new office staff—Janice, Terry, Maria, and Nicki. As I shook hands with each new person, I noted that they were friendly and warm. Maria hugged me tightly and said, "I'm so honored to meet you."

Trent heard all the fuss and walked into the office.

"Hey, Amy," he said when he saw me, "how are you?"

"I'm good, Trent," I said, shaking hands with him. I was grinning from ear to ear.

"You look different," he said tilting his head to look at me and taking a step back to study my appearance.

"I am different," I said succinctly.

"Let's go into my office. I want to catch up," Trent said. I was happily surprised that his office, the one that used to be mine for more than a decade, didn't stir my heart with any emotion.

"Trent," I said, "where did you put all the paper?" I asked looking around at his rather tidy and empty office, free of file cabinets and boxes of documents.

"Paper? Oh, you mean the work stuff. It's filed in the other office," he said. Yes! That's better, I thought recalling Beverly's crazy filing system.

I looked around my old office. On his bookshelf were some nutrition books that I'd left when I moved out. On the top shelf was a baseball cap that I designed, personally paid for, and gave to all two hundred staff as my good-bye present. It was in the university colors: a dark blue cap with gold lettering

Initially I planned to print "We Are the Champions!" in gold lettering but Ginny convinced me that the younger staff wouldn't know the song by Queen. So I stuck to the tried and true, our UC program logo.

Trent and I sat down. He sat behind his desk, and I sat in a chair across from him. He looked at me seriously and asked how I was feeling.

"I heard it's been rough for you," he said sadly.

"Thanks, Trent, for your support, but really, I'm fine," I said.

"You must have been devastated when they removed you from office," Trent said coming right to the point. He looked at me sadly, trying his best to be compassionate.

I thought about letting his comment go, but changed my mind.

"Ah, Trent," I said, "I wasn't removed from office. I voluntary returned to my faculty position."

"Same thing," he said, and waving his arms in the air indicating that he didn't really care.

Pity, it was going to be impossible to change the gossip now. I didn't argue; in fact, I decided to let the whole thing go and leaned back in my chair.

"So how do you like being director?" I said, changing the subject. "Are you mixing well with the faculty here?"

Trent told me that his position didn't include an academic assignment. He wasn't a member of the department.

"The director job is complex enough," Trent stated, his voice a little dry. "The position is totally administrative. No research," he stammered.

He cleared his throat. I assumed he wanted to talk to me about something that was bothering him. I waited.

"These program folks aren't happy with all the paperwork," he warbled. "They don't seem to get it. They complain that there are so many rules, and so much documentation," he said looking weary.

"Yes," I said nervously. "But there's no other option for that," I finished, feeling oh-so-glad not to be involved.

"Well, all I can say is," he said taking a deep breath, "it is what it is." I was thinking about my new role at UC. I had a reasonable job that didn't include frustrated people, long hours, and working like a dog.

"Good to see you," I said, getting up from the chair.

"Nice to see you too, Amy," he said smiling.

I shut the door, feeling grateful that this was his future and not mine. No question about it, I'd gotten out at the right time!

Ginny and I walked out to the coffee kiosk near the building. We bought our coffee and went to sit down on a bench in the shade to enjoy the moment and chat about the rest of our lives.

"How are you, Ginny?" I asked.

"I'm good," she told me. She looked happy and relaxed.

"So, how's work going? Is everything back to normal now?" I asked, gazing at the Food, Health and Society building in the distance.

"It is what it is," Ginny said laughing.

"Ginny, what on earth does that mean?" I said puzzled.

"Trent's been saying that ever since he returned from that bike ride," Ginny said amused.

"Oh yeah," I said, "the bike ride! I forgot that he did the ride from San Francisco to Los Angeles to raise money for the San Francisco AIDs Foundation," I said. "I was one of his many sponsors." I kicked myself for having forgotten to ask him about it.

"How'd he do?" I asked.

"He finished! Which is pretty darn great for someone who's never done a bike ride before," she said enthusiastically.

"Wow," I answered. "It is . . ."

"It is what it is . . ." Ginny finished my sentence for me

"I was going to say—it's amazing. Trent gets first place in my book."

We sat there as two ducks waddled by on the path to the creek that runs through Davis. Closely behind them followed a flock of little ones, trying so hard to keep up. The father, leading the way, seemed in a big hurry. The babies, fluffy and cute, were stumbling and tripping over each other with their tiny webbed feet. I wanted to scoop the last one up and help him along. He was dawdling, meandering, and falling behind, obviously the runt of the pack. I was worried that he'd be left behind to fend for itself. He was way too little to know any better.

"Ginny," I said standing up suddenly, "that baby duckling may need some help." I was ready to take action.

"Amy, wait," she said laughing and pulling me back to the bench. "He's going to be okay," she said.

Ginny, always the voice of reason, squeezed my hand affectionately. "Don't worry. He won't be left behind." I sat back down.

"So how's Judith?" Ginny asked as we watched the rest of the little ones parading along, attempting to get into a straight line.

"She's loving college life, especially now that her boyfriend, Damon, is back from his year abroad in Paris. He's a keeper," I told Ginny, "a real gentleman and so protective."

"And your grandkids?" I asked her. "How old are they now? Time seems to have slipped by so quickly! We can only mark time by our children," I said.

Ginny shared stories of her daughter and four grandchildren who'd moved in with her.

"The youngest is two and she's a handful. Everyone else is doing great—things are finally falling into place," Ginny told me. "It's nice to have a full house again," she said winking at me. I knew what she meant. After the kids leave the nest everything is so quiet.

"The kids are so cute. I love 'em to pieces," she said then admitted, "But oh, it's so exhausting!"

We heard the mother duck squawking directions at her crew. I imagined she was telling them to hurry up and get going—they, too, had a lot of things that need to be done. The small one at the end was so far behind now. He haphazardly turned himself around and was now moving in the wrong direction!

"That mother duck is really moving them along," Ginny commented.

"I got a feeling," I said pointing to the mother, "that she's one of those modern mom ducks—no nonsense! But the little one," I pointed again to the fuzziest one of the lot, "he needs his mother more than ever."

Next thing we know, the mom duck has rushed to the aid of the littlest one, who'd fallen off the path completely. She got behind him squawking and squealing and making a racket. She hustled and pushed him right back to the end of the line. He managed to catch up with the rest of the crew, and they all waddled away down the path together.

On June 10 I was given a key to my new office. The dean's office had moved all my stuff for me, and I spent the morning unpacking my personal knickknacks. I took Matt, my faculty friend from the retirement party, over to see it on our way to lunch. I couldn't believe how much time had passed. Matt's wavy blond hair was hidden under a baseball hat.

"Where's the building?" Matt asked, teasing me.

"My office is the building; it stands alone. Look, I no longer need a set of separate building and room keys, I just have the one," I smiled, dangling my one key in front of him.

I opened the door and we walked in. The cool air conditioning and simple wood furniture with a computer and books on the shelf conveyed tranquility. I could hear the cooing of doves nearby.

"Where are all your boxes?" Matt asked, looking around with a smile. Matt had seen my director office at the peak of the investigation. Crammed full of boxes with elaborate labels, my old office had resembled a police station evidence locker.

"No more boxes," I laughed, recalling the past. Showing Matt my daughter's high school graduation photo, I gazed at my shell collection on the window sill. The sun was peeking through the branches of a sturdy oak tree.

"Life's a lot simpler," I said turning out the lights as we headed out.

We drove to the *Ket MoRee*, a Thai restaurant in Davis, to escape the 110 degree heat. At the restaurant, which wasn't very busy, we ordered some very spicy curry and a tall Thai beer. Matt asked about my new life in Environmental Horticulture.

"Have you had any faculty meetings?" he said teasing me.

"Not yet," I answered. "You know, Matt," I said thinking out loud, "there really isn't an Environmental Horticulture Department anymore. I'm the only faculty member in the dean's office, so if a faculty meeting is ever convened it's likely to be short."

"Gawd, you're lucky," he said grinning.

I beamed. It was nice to be back.

The beer arrived, and I poured some in a glass for myself and passed the bottle to Matt. I raised my glass and we toasted our budding friendship.

"I finally figured out what happened," Matt said after taking a sip of his frosty beer.

"You blew the whistle on Beverly for falsifying travel and buying junk for herself," he began.

"Expensive junk—to the tune of $160,000!" I added.

Matt continued. "Fred didn't want you to blow the whistle because he didn't want his friend Raymond to get in trouble for misappropriation of grant funds."

"Yep, that's my take," I said taking a sip of the beer.

"Raymond may not have profited personally from all this," I said slowly to allow the idea to sink in, "but he didn't follow proper procedures when he protected Beverly," I concluded.

"I've been trying to stay blessedly unaware," Matt said, putting his hat on the table, "but I have to admit, I'm speechless."

I decided it was time to tell Matt exactly how I felt.

"For me," I said boldly, "I'm still pondering how anyone could feel OK about spending the money—money for poor families—to do their own research."

Matt picked up his glass and swirled the beer round and round.

"And if Raymond thought his research was so deserving—why not just say so?"

Matt eagerly dove back into the conversation, his cobalt eyes darting back and forth.

"Ah, come on, remember you're talking about Raymond," he said, stroking his beard and looking a little amused.

I flashed back at my first meeting with Raymond—the youthful superstar fiercely determined to make his department the very best.

"Maybe I'm old-fashioned, Matt," I said now sitting up straight, "but a ton of bigwigs from the university knew this was going on—why didn't anyone come forward?

"For example," I pressed on, "after Beverly was put on investigatory leave, Fred told me that he heard from someone that Beverly did the same thing at her previous job—Intel, IBM, or Apple—I don't actually remember which one."

"Hey, time out!" Matt said laughing loudly. "Are you telling me that Fred told you she was stealing *before* she came to Davis?"

"Yep. However, don't quote me—remember the scoop's from Fred and he might have iced the cake a bit," I giggled. "Fred was always my best source of information. He told me that Beverly was fired from her previous job for something similar. You know," I added, "I found out recently that she didn't have a master's degree—and I even wonder about all the other stuff she told us. She's not a big fan of the truth," I said, shaking my head.

"But letting people off the hook means that they're just going to keep doing it," I called out.

"Well, the university pulled out their cannons on her this time around," Matt announced refilling his glass with the rest of the bottle.

I nodded with gratitude.

"Speaking of getting away with it, Fred knew what was going on," Matt stated. "He told everyone. He just wanted the whole thing to be handled at a departmental level," Matt added.

"He probably didn't think I'd blow the whistle," I said.

"I bet Fred's been kicking himself about that!" Matt answered.

"I'm often asked if I'd do it again," I said reflectively. "The answer is yes, in a heartbeat!"

"And what advice do you have for others who might be tempted to follow in your footsteps," Matt said, pretending to hold up a microphone for me to speak into.

"Well, Matt," I said seriously, "I'd tell the next whistleblower that they'll have no choice. It's not something you can turn your back on. You will do it and you won't regret doing it," I answered putting the joking aside for a minute.

"It's the next part that's hard," I continued. "You have to decide how much you're willing to put their life on hold. After blowing the whistle, you need to hunker down and prepare for the fight of your life. How long can you handle the difficulties?

Resolution will take many years. Are you willing to wait four years or more? That's a long time. You'll be frustrated, taunted, vilified, terrified; you'll likely lose your friends and many will hate you. The isolation will be painful. You won't receive an award, monetary or otherwise, and you may never get thanked. And if you do get thanked for blowing the whistle, it will be treated like a giant secret."

I so much wanted to tell Matt about the letter I recently received from the vice-provost and the one from the chancellor a few months before. Sadly, I wasn't supposed to discuss the content with anyone until the investigation was over.

"But personally, the hardest part will be all the time you spend trying to understand," I finished.

"So, do you understand?" Matt asked looking me in the eye, now serious too.

"Absolutely! It's fairly simple. There are some bad people in places that you'd least expect. Unable to see past their own self-interests, these people are arrogant and greedy; they lie and deceive; some are miserable swags, and some just plain thugs."

"You're beginning to sound a lot like Hamlet," Matt said teasingly.

"A knavish speech sleeps in a foolish ear," I answered swiftly. "There are also many good people." I smiled, thinking about Dan Ellsberg and others at Davis. "You have to get back on your feet and find them!" I said, momentarily pausing as I visualized my childhood self clinging to the rock, waiting to be rescued.

Matt clapped his hands and I bowed.

"What have you been doing lately?" Matt asked me.

"During my year away from the department, I served on some national committees and I wrote a paper which has been accepted for publication next January. It's back to business for me," I answered.

"Oh, and here's my business card," I said, handing Matt my newly printed card with my new title and address in Environmental Horticulture. On the top corner of the card was the university's golden seal.

"Hey, hold it up to the light," I suggested. "You'll see the picture of a whistle embossed on the card," I suggested.

Matt held it up to the light and looked puzzled.

"I'm kidding," I said, then I paused and added, "I guess I should stop making whistleblower jokes."

"You should stop making *silly* whistleblower jokes," Matt said looking at me sideways.

Our food arrived and we stopped talking to enjoy the yellow Thai curry. Everything tasted especially wonderful, the potatoes, avocado, and carrots oozing in curry spices, coconut, and chicken. We both dug into a heaping plate as the steam rose above the flavorful concoction.

"Enough about me," I announced with gratitude. "How's your work going?"

"Well, I haven't been around much," Matt said honestly.

"Why's that?" I asked hooking a mass of gooey curry onto my chopsticks.

Matt told me that it was annoying to hear everyone grumbling and bickering about the Beverly-thing.

"People were bellowing and picking fights," he told me. "Seeing Beverly's buddies cruising the hallways looking for sympathy was a drag," he explained.

"Now that she's history, my chums do seem calmer," he admitted. "Fred and Raymond aren't around much and no one seems to care," he snickered. "Personally I'm happy that I don't have to hear them sulking in the mail room broadcasting their woes to everyone who walks by," Matt blurted out. "It's a relief not to hear the riffraff belly-aching about what a raw deal they got. Raymond seems not to have the 'distinguished professor' title any more!" Matt snickered. I pictured Raymond's Web site with an "undistinguished professor" caption under his photo.

"So, are things better ... ?" I asked, wondering if anything had changed four years later.

"Well, it depends on what you mean by better," he answered

thoughtfully. "I have to admit there's a lot of extra work on tracking financial records and getting approvals," he said sighing. "But, at least we know that the money is being used properly . . . geez I never thought I'd say that!"

We both sat there reflecting on Matt's statement that things were better.

"Matt, thank you for all your support," I said softly.

"Hey," he answered smiling at me, his eyes twinkling with appreciation. "You did good."

On June 17, 2009, I walked into Mrak Hall and headed straight to the dean's office, where the MOU I'd discussed with Dean Fitzgerald was waiting for my signature. As I opened the glass doors, I momentarily recalled my past life. My eyes brightened as I turned the corner to stop and read the university's "Principles of Community" hanging on the entrance wall.[15]

This time when I read it, I felt the elegance and grace and was moved by the simplicity of the credo it evoked. "The University of California, Davis, is first and foremost an institution of learning and teaching, committed to serving the needs of society . . . We affirm the inherent dignity in all of us, and we strive to maintain a climate of justice . . . We will strive to build a true community of spirit and purpose based on mutual respect and caring."

I found myself thinking forward this time. I wasn't haunted by the need to look over my shoulder to see who might be watching.

I was ready to face life's uncertainties with the same equanimity that got me here.

At 11:30 a.m., I signed the MOU. I signed it with sincerity, then walked back to my new office, strolling through the arboretum. It was a lovely summer day. A ray of sun sparkled on a group of visitors whose laughter rang through the manicured gardens.

I wasn't born a whistleblower. Like those before me, I just did what I believed was right. And this was good enough.

Notes

1. Johnny Mercer, *Moon River* (Nashville, Tennessee: Sony ATV Harmony, 1961).

2. Michael J. Fox is an actor in the *Back to the Future* movies from Universal Pictures, Los Angeles, California, 1985 and 1989.

3. Margaret Randall, Muriel S. Brink, and Amy B. Joy, "EFNEP: An Investment in America's Future," *Journal of Nutrition Education*, 21 (6): 276-279, 1989.

4. Martin Yan, *Culinary Journey Through China* (San Francisco: KQED Books, 1996).

5. The actual name of the company has been changed.

6. Personal letter, March 2, 2006.

7. Amy Block Joy, *Whistleblower Report* University of California, Davis, California, August 25, 2006.

8. Ibid.

9. Personal letter, February 23, 2007.

10. Daniel Ellsberg, *Secrets: A Memoir of Vietnam and the Pentagon Papers* (New York: Viking Penguin, 2002).

11. K. Lloyd Billings, "Food for Fraud," *Capital Ideas* 12 (17), Sacramento, April 24, 2007.

12. C. Fred Alford, *Whistleblowers: Broken Lives and Organizational Power* (New York: Cornell University Press, 2001).

13. James Brown, *I Got You I Feel Good* (New York, New York: Fort Knox Music, 1965).

14. Cole Porter, *I've Got You Under My Skin* (Santa Monica, California: Chappell and Co, Inc., 1956).

15. Office of the Vice Chancellor, "Principles of Community," University of California, Davis, 2003.

Acknowledgments

I want to thank the many people who stood beside me over the past four years.

Heartfelt thanks to my daughter, Judith. "I wish you all the joy that you can wish" (*Merchant of Venice*, Shakespeare). Your creative spirit is exhilarating to behold. Thank you for your daily phone calls, and for sharing your life with me.

During the development of this book, I was honored to be guided by a talented consultant. My developmental editor, Alan Rinzler, was the inspiring voice who taught me the healing power of words. Alan provided honest feedback as he kept me focused and moving forward. I'm forever grateful to you for sharing this journey with me.

And to David Cole, my savvy Bay Tree Publishing publisher extraordinaire, thank you. Your clarity, enthusiasm, and dedication to this project brought this book to life. I cherish our work together.

I am eternally grateful to my team of attorneys. Special thanks to my insightful and talented whistleblower attorney, Michael A. Hirst, Esq., who stood by my side with his unwavering support and to my literary attorney, Eric Rayman, Esq.

To my friends, thank you for encouraging me through thick and thin, for your endless generosity and unflappable support. I wanted to list you each by name but was worried that you might not want to be listed since none of you knew about this book—and, by the way, I love you!

Thank you Ida for your support and encouragement over

the years. And Shari, my friend and writing buddy from Taos, thank you for keeping me sane all these years! I have a handful of brave colleagues from the university who still speak to me—thank you for your humanity.

I want to thank the investigators and other folks who I worked with at the University of California, Davis. Thank you for asking all the tough questions, for treating me fairly and equally, and for making sure that my legal rights were maintained. Your professional ethics and personal integrity were of the highest level, and I'm honored to have worked with you.

Thanks, as well, to my copyeditor, Katherine Silver, who, with very sharp skill, trimmed, cut, and fitted the manuscript down to size. I'm going to wear this book with pride.

I wish to acknowledge the creative work on the book cover: Mary Lee Cole for her cover design and photographer Barrie Rokeach.

I want to pay tribute to those who walked with me, especially my buddy Ginny Buckner who made numerous personal sacrifices as we strove to make the world a better place.

And to Matt—a composite of four brave university folks who spoke to me—thank you!

And finally, a wish and plea to all future whistleblowers: please know that it is very possible to look back and say, "Yes! I am glad I blew the whistle."